BUILDING FOR TOMORROW

THE AGA KHAN AWARD FOR ARCHITECTURE
BUILDING FOR TOMORROW

Edited by Azim A Nanji

ACADEMY EDITIONS

ACKNOWLEDGEMENTS

This volume would not have been possible without the collaboration of Jalal Uddin Ahmed of the Islamic Arts Foundation, and editor of Arts and the Islamic World. *His initiative, interest and support have been invaluable throughout the preparation of the work.*

I would like to record my thanks to the staff of the Aga Khan Award for Architecture and the Secretary General, Dr Suha Özkan for their assistance in providing illustrations and access to material. I would also like to extend my gratitude to Susan Lewis and Shireen Karmali, and to Andrea Bettella, Mario Bettella, Ramona Khambatta, and Toby Norman at Academy Editions for their assistance in the final preparation of the manuscript.

PHOTOGRAPHIC CREDITS

PAGE 2: Reha Günay
THE AGA KHAN AWARD FOR ARCHITECTURE: Kamran Adle, Mohamed Akram, A Bennys, Jacques Bétant, Cemal Emden, Reha Günay, Christian Lignon, Christopher Little, Suha Özkan, Pehlivanoglu
THINKING ARCHITECTURE: Christopher Little
WRITING ON THE ARCHITECTURE OF ISLAM: Christopher Little
THE TANGLED WEB OF TIME: Kamran Adle, Khedija M'Hadhebi, James Steele
THOUGHTS ON ARCHITECTURE: Cemal Emden, Christina Emden
CONSERVATION IN THE ISLAMIC WORLD: Jacques Bétant, Christopher Lignon
EXPRESSING AN ISLAMIC IDENTITY: Gulzar Haider, Wolfgang Hoyt courtesy of Skidmore Owings Merrill, Aldo Ippoliti, James Steele
REHABILITATION OF KSOUR, DRAA VALLEY, MOROCCO: Christian Lignon
THE ARCHEOLOGICAL AND ARCHITECTURAL HERITAGE OF EAST AFRICA: CM Chama
THE SOCIAL CHALLENGE TO MODERN ISLAMIC ARCHITECTURE: Gregorius Antar, Chant Avedissian
THE AGA KHAN PROGRAM FOR ISLAMIC ARCHITECTURE: Reha Günay
INTENTIONS AND CHALLENGES: Chant Avedissian, Pascal Marechaux, Skidmore Owings Merrill
THE AGA KHAN AWARD FOR ARCHITECTURE: A CRITICAL COMMENTARY: Pascal Marechaux, Reha Günay, Kamran Adle
JOURNEY TO SAMARKAND: Reha Günay
COURAGEOUS CRITERIA: Kamran Adle
TALK BY HIS HIGHNESS THE AGA KHAN: Jacques Bétant
ANOTHER MOORE: The Collection of Moore Ruble Yudell

Cover: *Aga Khan Award for Architecture, 1983, Hajj Terminal, Jeddah, Saudi Arabia*
Page 2: *Aga Khan Award for Architecture, 1989, National Assembly Building, Dhaka, Bangladesh*
Page 6: *Aga Khan Award for Architecture, 1989, Al-Kindi Plaza, Riyadh, Saudi Arabia*
Page 7: *Gur-i Amir, Samarkand*
Page 8: *Aga Khan Award for Architecture, 1989, Institut du Monde Arabe*

Editorial Offices
42 Leinster Gardens London W2 3AN

First published in Great Britain in 1994 by
ACADEMY EDITIONS
An imprint of Academy Group Ltd

ACADEMY GROUP LTD
42 Leinster Gardens London W2 3AN
Member of the VCH Publishing Group

ISBN 1 85490 393 4

Distributed to the trade in the United States of America by
ST MARTIN'S PRESS
175 Fifth Avenue, New York, NY 10010

Printed and bound in Italy

CONTENTS

ENABLING CONVERSATIONS

Azim A Nanji

For most of the twentieth century, the focal point of global tensions was assumed to be the ideological border between East and West, the former Soviet Union and its allies against Western democracies. The implications and consequences of the conflict reverberated across a constantly changing map of the world. The emergence of new tensions in the post-Cold War era has caused recent theorists and observers to shift the focus elsewhere and to imagine new enemies. One such divide, according to this view, is a clash between emerging civilisation clusters. In this revised geography, one such global conflict pits an imagined and homogeneous Western political culture and space against a Muslim one. The most accessible model for understanding human destiny, according to this equation, is a continuing series of dichotomised cultural/national spaces and a new duality that makes it easier to view a polarised world as still inhabited by fixed and irreconcilable differences. Rethinking a complex evolving global environment in which a sense of difference may exist, without being threatening, is much harder.

As the essays in this retrospective on the Aga Khan Award for Architecture suggest, there is a transnational and transterritorial 'landscape' out of which a constructive discourse can emerge. Through a definition of architecture that engages the whole built environment and situates human and cultural concerns at the heart of the conversation about the future of building in the Muslim world, the Award has led, initiated and sustained an enabling series of conversations. It has created new avenues for inquiry about architecture and illuminated some of the shifts that have occurred during the period of the Award. It has developed reference points and a record of achievements to address the concerns, needs and aspirations of architects, clients, governments, educators, communities and others in lands where Muslims live and work. The presentations, programmes, publications, seminars and networks resulting from the Award are international in scope. They point to the creative role of architecture and challenge assumptions about the perceived homogeneity of Islamic architectural heritage. For some, the development of 'modern' architecture may still be the fundamental concern of twentieth-century architecture, but it is no longer possible to exclude from a broad discussion, the range of architectural directions and trends in other parts of the world, including the Muslim world. Thus, one of the enabling aspects of the Award has been to provide a space in which a global dialogue can take place and where multi-narratives find a forum for expression. Such simultaneous conversations have led to the acknowledgement that local, regional and vernacular forms of architecture may play a positive role in times of rapid and often chaotic change.

In general, awards in the field of architecture and design provide indices of what is appealing, what is to be preferred and the directions indicated in the determination of taste. The Aga Khan Award for Architecture has tried to go further than that. It has provoked debate that can be sustained beyond the rewards, by encouraging a search for intellectual, ethical and practical directions and by linking its purposes to the needs of people in the developing world, without assuming a parochial or doctrinaire position on how this might be attained. Particularly, in helping to define the meaning and role of architecture in Muslim contexts, the Award has enabled a broader multi-dimensional definition to emerge. Muslim architecture has been seen to be a conversation among many cultures and spaces in the past and in the present. It continues to be, as it has always been at its most creative moments, a negotiation, synthesis and interplay of all those spaces and traditions that transcend the idea of 'Islamic Architecture' as a monologue.

However, the existing fragmentation of architectural discourse and practice in the Muslim world and the realities of demographic, urban and social change add a certain urgency to the way in which one might rethink the built environment and in particular the exploding cities that mark the present era.

The essays in this volume, while different in focus and approach, indicate how the Award has fostered and forged such a 'community of concern'. This shared concern has led to a sense of mission and engagement to protect a tradition of cultural diversity for generations yet unborn, and develop options for the next century – not just for a fifth of humanity that is Muslim, but for the others among whom Muslims live and increasingly share the task of building for tomorrow.

Aga Khan Award for Architecture, 1983, Shah Rukn-i-'Alam Mausoleum, Multan, Pakistan

THE AGA KHAN AWARD FOR ARCHITECTURE

The Anatomy of an Approach to Promoting Architectural Excellence

Ismail Serageldin

Few enterprises in the world of architecture generally, and in the world of Islam specifically, have made as serious an effort at establishing a critical foundation for the improvement of the built environment as the Aga Khan Award for Architecture.[1] The scope of the vision is breathtaking: to elevate the consciousness of the decision makers and the professionals that create an impact on the built environment of Muslims through the selection of outstanding examples of contemporary architecture for, or by, the Muslim people in the world today, granting them international recognition. Such consciousness-raising would then translate into a greater commitment to quality on the part of those whose decisions create an impact on the built environment, resulting in better buildings and a better built environment.

Ambitious as such a project is, it was made even more so by the decision of the Award not to embrace a single architectural 'style' as 'the' solution. It decided instead to promote a wide range of approaches, provided that they met certain criteria of integrity and intrinsic quality, in order not to stifle creativity or to unjustly limit the necessary variety of architectural responses that are suitable for as varied a constituency as the Muslim people.

If that is the vision, how far has the Award succeeded in meeting these lofty objectives? How effective has the Award been in changing the approach being followed in the Muslim world? What did the Award's efforts produce as a contribution to the architectural profession and architectural criticism? This essay tries to address these questions, and in the process will raise some queries on the meaning of identity in a developing and rapidly-changing world, as well as the role of architecture and architects in the midst of societies in social transformation.

To better understand the limitations and successes of the Award, it is pertinent to assess first the realities of the context in which the Award works, and how appropriate the response was of the Award to the issues raised by the interaction of the Award's objectives and the milieu in which it operates.

1. The Setting

Let us start by reviewing the milieu in which the Award's activities are expected to produce a profound impact. The Muslim world, or what could be more appropriately called the world of the Muslim societies of today, is a world that generally remains economically disadvantaged and is made up predominantly of poorer developing countries, heavily weighted by the populations of South and South-East Asia. It is mostly rural, although urbanisation is accelerating at a rate unparalleled since the Industrial Revolution. It is also being swept by immense changes which have generated tension and conflict due to the ongoing and painful process of evolving a truly contemporary, yet authentic sense of self-identity.

To circumscribe the Muslim world more specifically is not as easy as it may initially seem, since several ways of defining it exist. The forty-four countries which have sent representatives to the Islamic Conference, for example, do not include huge Muslim minorities in India, China or some of the republics of the former Soviet Union which represents more than 200 million people, but do include countries such as Ethiopia and Lebanon. These countries illustrate the main point, however, that the Muslim world is extremely heterogeneous. It stretches from Morocco to Indonesia, and at the start of this decade embraced close to a billion people. The nation states involved range in area from Bahrain, at 1,000 km² to the 2.5 million km² of Sudan; in population from the 524,000 of Qatar to close to 190 million in Indonesia, in per capita income from the miserable average of the equivalent of around $200 annually in Bangladesh, Chad and Somalia (which are among the poorest countries in the world) to the over $20,000 annual income in Kuwait, Brunei, and the United Arab Emirates (which are the richest countries in the developing world), using the same criteria. Such averages, which admittedly obliterate subtle, and not so subtle differences, reveal a Muslim world that is 4.5 times the area of the United States, and has three times as many people, but significantly, only six per cent of its per capita income, the equivalent of about $800 to $900 a year.

This world is, then, sometimes rich but mostly poor, in which almost half of the population, demographically weighted in the large countries of Bangladesh, Pakistan, Indonesia and Nigeria, fall in the lower-middle income or low income sector internationally. One of the key concerns within such nations is to modernise the economic base while improving the standard of living of the people. What the West had the luxury of achieving sequentially,

FROM ABOVE: Aga Khan Award for Architecture (AKAA), 1989, Rehabilitation of Asilah, Asilah, Morocco; AKAA, 1989, Grameen Bank Housing Project, Dhaka, Bangladesh; OVERLEAF: Interior of the restored summer palace of Khedive Abbas Hilmi Pasha II, located on the Asian shore of Istanbul, in Cubuklu

beginning with the organisation of industrial production, followed by concern for the social welfare of the citizenry, the developing world must somehow manage to do concurrently, for it is unacceptable today that the horrors of the Industrial Revolution and the England of Dickens could be re-enacted with the consent and support of the governments concerned.

Today the prevalent idea is to promote both economic and social welfare simultaneously, usually looking to the industrialised Western countries as the model, leading to the widespread acceptance of the idea that progress is synonymous with 'Westernisation'. This, in turn, has contributed to the cultural bifurcation visible in many Muslim countries today, which can be directly attributed to accelerated socio-economic development. The majority of the vast constituency which the Aga Khan Award for Architecture seeks to address, then, has basic concerns, similar to most developing countries, which are much more vital than those which preoccupy their post-industrial counterparts. These concerns include meeting the unrelenting challenge of providing shelter for the poor, numbering in the hundreds of millions. This extreme misery unfortunately affects as much as one third of the population of the Muslim world. These people, many of whom are children, are caught up in a condition of life so limited by malnutrition, disease, illiteracy, brief life-expectancy and high infant mortality, as to be beneath any rational definition of human decency. Half of them are found in South Asia, mainly in India and Bangladesh, another sixth in East and South-East Asia, mainly Indonesia, and a majority of the remainder in the Middle East and Sub-Saharan Africa.

This Muslim world is young, with about half the population under twenty-five years of age. It is growing rapidly and could reach as high a number as 1,200 million by the end of the century. Many of these people will live in very poor households crammed into cities already filled to overflowing – the Jakartas, Karachis, Teherans, Cairos and Lagoses of the Muslim world. The reality to be accepted is that, as far as the issue of basic survival and shelter is concerned, in the next decade the Muslim world will be bigger and more impoverished, with many more poor families in immediate need of basic shelter.

The Muslim world which I have described is, therefore, a world which is still quite poor. The glossy image projected by the new architecture of the oil producing countries should not be allowed to obscure this fact. It is not surprising that these societies seem to be drifting without purpose, as they navigate their way through a period of unprecedented transition.[2] It is axiomatic that the currents of internationalisation, and especially the influences of Western, industrialised nations, have had a powerful effect which has caused an identity crisis. This sense of a lack of purpose, being at the mercy of external forces, and being caught between a past which appears to be vanishing and an uncertain future, has generated undercurrents of tension, and indeed, open conflict. This has placed a burden of stress on the social fabric that is in direct proportion to the stress that may be identified in individual communities and the lives within them.

Although such forces have reached different levels of intensity and impact in various nations and regions of the Muslim world, few, if any, have escaped the consequences. Change, rather than stability, is thus the key factor in Muslim societies today, and even greater change can be anticipated in the future. This is the milieu in which the Award is operating.

2. The Award's Scope and Coverage

The choice of the approach taken by the Award to address the needs of architecture in this rapidly changing Muslim world had consequences for both the activities of the Award and its effectiveness. Clearly, opting for a slower but more profound approach was bound to result in a seeming lack of focus or clarity. It was an inevitable consequence of a strategic decision concerning how to influence creative processes, but nevertheless remain relevant to the needs of a rapidly changing society.

What then were the key attributes of this approach? To start with, the Award decided to eschew the promotion of a single architectural style or idea. In fact, the initial proposal was for a series of five prizes (see the first brochure for the Award dated 1977). The first master jury, in 1980 surprised the Award's Steering Committee by selecting fifteen projects as winners, and defining these as under seven themes. There was clearly a lot more to be covered than could be captured under the original five themes of prizes. Why? Because two sets of issues were at work here. These were articulated fully in August 1983 in a memorandum that outlined the approach to the Award that was to be reflected in the subsequent briefs to the master juries from 1986 onwards.[3]

The first set of issues refers to the scope of the Award. Indeed, to be relevant to the nature of the challenge faced by those who would deal with the built environment in the Muslim world, at least three different dimensions of the architectural challenge had to be addressed:
First, the need to protect the heritage, at risk of irretrievable loss in most of the Muslim countries of the world.
Second, the need to deal with the needs of the poor, in terms of shelter and other construction, for the Muslim world is remarkably poor in the aggregate.
Third, the need to address the creation of a new architectural vocabulary and language of expression for societies seeking to define themselves against the rapidly changing world around and within them.

There are of course many additional nuances within the various categories that bring an almost infinite richness to the array of problems that are to be treated within this already exceptionally vast scope.

The formal adoption of this tripartite definition of the scope of the Award's mandate was given eloquent expression in the address of His Highness the Aga Khan, at the Fourth Award Ceremony in Cairo in October 1989. As he said then:

> As we reflect on some of the Award's lessons of the last twelve years, three strong themes of concern have emerged: first, protection, restoration and skilful re-use of the heritage of the past, at a time when that heritage, the anchor of identity and source of our inspiration, is being threatened with destruction, by war and environmental degradation or by the inexorable demographic and economic pressures of exploding urban growth. Second, addressing the pressing needs for social development and community buildings in a Muslim world all too beset by mass poverty. Third, identifying in contemporary architectural expression, the best efforts at capturing the opportunities of the present and defining our dreams for tomorrow.[4]

The second set of issues pertains to the tremendous diversity of the societies that comprise the 'Muslim world'. What may serve as an example to the builders in the oil-rich countries of the Gulf, has no relevance to the poorest societies of the Sahel. Likewise, the tremendous climatic and geographic variety of the countries covered by the Award indicates the need for selecting a sufficient number of examples to enable each sub-region in this richly diversified world to find insights of direct relevance to them and to their problems.

These two sets of issues relating to the scope and to the coverage of the Award conspired to lead to the selection of a large number of winners, and furthermore, winners that did not at first blush, seem to have much in common. It required a special intellectual effort to read the meaning of the Award winners.[5] An effort that the architectural press, which oscillates between the superficial and the partisan, had exceptional difficulty with.

The lack of a clear message could have been remedied and even enhanced by replacing the absence of a simple clear choice with a clear approach to architectural criticism. It is here that the Award has failed in its communication strategy. For that is the key contribution that it makes both to the Muslim world and to the architectural profession. The Award is the most detailed and serious enterprise of its kind in the world. Yet that seriousness is not captured in the relatively short statements that accompany the announcement of the winners.[6] Only briefly had the Award started to do justice to its mission of architectural criticism,[7] when it sponsored the seminar on architectural criticism in Malta in 1987 [8] and the subsequent seminar on the expressions of Islam in buildings held in Indonesia in 1990.[9] But the lack of continuity in both presence and discourse made these appear as isolated events rather than parts of an ongoing search, which they were.

What were the constituent parts of this search? What was the underlying approach?

3. The Approach: A Space for Freedom

Having disposed of the questions of the scope and coverage of the Award's mandate, it is pertinent to turn to the Award's approach; specifically, its decision not to champion a single solution in any of the three themes or any specific part of the Muslim world. Instead, the Award chose to take a broad and tolerant approach that valued pluralism and diversity, and promoted debate and an ongoing 'search' rather than a 'solution'.[10] Was this decision, encapsulated in the title 'space for freedom' an appropriate one? What were the consequences, both positive and negative, of this decision? Let us review the application of the approach to each of the three themes, and discuss the validity of the approach as reflected in the selected winners within that special theme.

3.1 Confronting the Past

The importance of preserving the heritage of the past cannot be overstated. While we must accept that change and reuse are an integral part of cities and societies as living organisms, the wholesale destruction of the heritage that is taking place in many Muslim countries today is of a different character. It robs the world at large of an irreplaceable heritage, and robs future generations of Muslims of their patrimony. The pace of change in today's cities makes the fragile historic districts vulnerable as they have never been before. Everywhere, ferment and change have highlighted the necessity for the physical preservation and restoration of individual monuments and/or the conservation of historic areas.

We need, however, to distinguish between this appeal for the sensitive protection and reuse of the past and those who in many of the Muslim societies of today, seek to block what they consider a headlong rush into the future. They use the past as an anchor, as an assertion of individuality, with identity being established only by the outstanding paradigms of the past. What we are addressing here is the need to keep examples of the past as an essential constituent/element of the evolving identity, but only as one of the constituent elements. It is, however, an essential element. At the very least, where no 'great' examples are found, society typically seeks to enhance the relevance of those 'witnesses' of its history, no matter how modest, for they provide an element of continuity for an evolving self-identify.

In addressing this issue, the Award has again shown its commitment to its approach, and consequently reflects pluralism and variety in its chosen winners.

There are at least three ways of approaching historic conservation in the Muslim world today. These are area conservation, individual buildings and adaptive reuse. The Award chose to approach them all.[11] Yet, within each of these broad approaches to historic conservation, there are different implementation philosophies and the Award recognised outstanding examples of each. Let us look at the record:

Area Conservation: Arguably, it is the 'sense of place' that reflects the character of an area. It conveys its spirit and creates its charm. Nowhere is this more true than in many of the older districts and quarters where the individual buildings are nondescript or even mediocre, but where the whole is much more than the sum of the parts. The Award recognised this from the first, granting a well-earned prize to Sidi Bou Saïd in Tunisia, a tourist based 'village' where the character has been forcefully protected by legislation. That example, however, relied on gentrification and a tourist economic base to keep it functioning. Later prizes were to be awarded to different approaches in terms of institutional arrangements, but always without compromise on the final quality. Thus the now tragic city of Mostar was recognised for the mix of fiscal and institutional arrangements as well as the effectiveness of the restoration. Asilah in Morocco was the result of self-help schemes. There is no single right way to achieve great results.

Individual Monuments: Almost every Award cycle has yielded memorable examples of outstanding restoration of great monuments, none perhaps as moving and outstanding as the restoration of the al-Aqsa Mosque in Jerusalem. But the logic of the Award's approach is best captured in the three winners selected in 1983. The Shah-Rukni-'Alam Mausoleum in Multan, Pakistan was a remarkable example of restoring a monument to its old grandeur, where the new cannot be easily distinguished from the old (but is carefully marked for the specialists). The Darb Qirmiz restoration was careful to leave the distinctions between the new and the old clear. The Azem Palace in Damascus was a total reconstruction, incorporating elements from entirely different buildings of the same period. All three were superb in the resulting effect, but clearly represent different schools of restoration.

By refusing to take a definitive stand on the narrow technical questions of how the restoration was done, the Award was stressing its commitment to the broader issue of the importance of safeguarding these examples of the past to enrich the present and the future.

Adaptive Reuse: Ultimately, this is the manifestation of a living city or society. Several examples have won awards, including the restoration of the Rustëm Pasa Caravanserai in Edirne, Turkey; the Ertegun house in Bodrum, Turkey; and the historic sites development of the Turkish touring club, as well as the reuse of the Azem Palace as a museum. The breadth of the Award's selected winners from area conservation, individual monuments or adaptive reuse underscores an important philosophical point. It

FROM ABOVE: AKAA, 1986, Mostar Old Town, Yugoslavia; AKAA, 1980, Sidi Bou Saïd Village, Tunis, Tunisia; OVERLEAF: AKAA, 1989, exterior and interior view of the Corniche Mosque, Jeddah, Saudi Arabia

opens avenues for the architects to do more than restore the buildings of the past, or even to imaginatively reuse them. Indeed, if the skills of architects in a society deal only with the physical preservation of building, space or urban character, they will prove inadequate. Architects must also acquire a level of sophistication in the ability to read the symbolic content of the heritage in a way that enriches their ability to produce relevant buildings for today and tomorrow, and guide 'authentification' efforts between the twin dangers of ossified copying of the past and cultural inappropriateness. This kind of slavish adherence to the past and its decorative details has been the downfall of a recently discredited historical style widely criticised for superficiality and irrelevance.

The sophistication needed to avoid a similar direction in the future and the discounting of value mentioned by Robert Venturi in *Plus Ça Change* (in which he compares the loss of validity in Post-Modernism to that in the Modernist Gestalt that preceded it, for the same reason, of falling into the hands of less talented practitioners) can come only through a strengthened educational process.[12] This will, in future, engender architects the critical capacity required to decode the symbolic content of the past in a realistic – as opposed to an overly theoretical or ideologically charged – way. It will necessitate a broad knowledge of the methodology as well as the factual reality of historical studies, an awareness of the present realities of Muslim societies, and an ability to innovate by a process of successive attempts at integration. The Award's contributions to this kind of educational enterprise is considerable – if only the clarity of the theoretical foundations of the Award's work were better known and understood.

3.2 Responding to the Needs of People and Society

No discipline can claim that it is relevant to society if it does not address its major problems. In the case of practitioners dealing with the built environment of the Muslim world, we must address the abysmal poverty and destitution which affects the mass of people. Improvements in their built environment through infrastructure improvements and the provision of shelter are valuable if they are replicable and succeed in empowering the local communities in being the producers of their own welfare and bounty, rather than the recipients of charity or aid.

Over the years the winners of the Award have shown diversity and consistency – the original choice of the Kampung Improvement Programme in Jakarta being a real example. Subsequent winners also emphasised the urban problems of the poor – the Surabaya Kampung Improvement Programme and the Chitra Nianga Programme for commercial development in Indonesia. Others, such as Ismailiyya in Egypt addressed the self-help approach of peri-urban settlements. The Grameen Housing Programme was a notable winner for addressing the needs of the rural poor in a most effective fashion.

All these winners raised different questions for architectural critics everywhere, since the traditional aesthetic criteria of judging buildings do not normally apply. Yet, the Award enriched the very meaning of architecture by raising this kind of activity to the level of recognition normally afforded only to the large-scale Architecture with a capital 'A'.

3.3 Inventing the Future

In the end, however, the Award has also made and continues to make a major contribution in the more mainstream intellectual area of the quality of contemporary architectural expression. It is in this area that the nuances and subtleties of its unique approach need the most clarification, for it is here that the Award confronted the most established and entrenched positions in architectural criticism. It is also here that the Award has confronted the partisanship of competing 'schools' of architecture. While the conservation and the social themes may have surprised and nonplussed the architectural critics, they did not feel necessarily equipped to debate the merits of these choices. But when it came to contemporary architectural expression, it was open season on the Award. This requires explanation, for the Award's choice of promoting a critical approach as a long-term strategy as opposed to championing a particular viewpoint, was frequently misunderstood.

4. Anchoring the Approach in a Methodology:
4.1 A Tired and Tiresome Debate

The greatest contribution of the Award was to avoid getting sucked into the sterile 'Modernity vs Tradition' debate – a tired and tiresome debate. In practically every forum dealing with contemporary Muslim societies, someone can always be counted upon to frame the issues under discussion in the form of a dichotomous relationship between 'Tradition' (usually presented as harmonious and wonderful) and 'Modernity' (usually presented as alienating, dehumanising and awful). Someone can also be counted upon to immediately reverse the dichotomy, arguing that Muslim societies cannot live in the past and that modernity (here presented as science, technology and progress) is the future. This debate is not only technically and critically flawed (if not outright wrong), but it is also highly unproductive and even counterproductive. The debate is unproductive because it usually leads to endless repetition and the marshalling of ever more examples and highly selective anecdotal evidence to buttress the *a priori* positions. The debate is also counterproductive because it tends to raise passions and make critical rational discourse even more difficult than it already is.

That this debate is technically flawed derives from the simplistic reductionism implicit in the dichotomous position: as if the rich tapestry representing the historical experience of the Muslim people could be reduced to a single 'tradition' (or traditional position in the debate), or that modernity – a complex, evolving concept that is highly relative and intertwined with contemporaneity – could be conveniently circumscribed into a single definable reality applicable from Morocco to Indonesia and from China to Africa.

It is also critically flawed because it does not use the tools of criticism to expand our understanding of the issues involved. Without such an expanded understanding, we are unlikely to progress beyond the repetitious, sterile litanies of this tired and tiresome debate. It was the Award's mission to develop an alternative, critical approach to the issues.

4.2 The Real Issues

If we set aside the simplistic dichotomous presentation of 'modernity' and 'tradition', we should start with the recognition that Muslim societies, each with its own unique specificities as well as shared commonalities, are everywhere in different stages of transformation, moving at vastly differing paces, although the rapidity and accelerating rate of change is a common feature. These changes, occurring under the pressure of demographic growth, rural-urban shifts and structural changes in the productive economic bases of the societies concerned, are also linked to global and international trends in myriad ways. Such changes must have profound socio-cultural manifestations which are reflected in the architecture of the contemporary Muslim societies. Most important among these manifestations is a sense of loss of 'cultural identity'.

Few issues have affected contemporary Muslim societies as deeply as this sense of loss of identity[13] and the corollary search for cultural authenticity which runs through much of the artistic, as well as the socio-political, activities in the Muslim world. Some have adopted an approach that seeks to return to the fountainhead of the Islamic faith to redefine the Muslim culture in its 'essential' terms, usually meaning a return to a (mythical) past which history, Western hegemony and geographic realities have introduced.[14] This approach is too narrow, overly romantic,[15] and fundamentally nonhistorical. Instead, the Award sought to thoroughly understand the past and to decode its language through contemporary eyes that can sift the relevant from the timebound. The arsenal of contemporary analysis was brought to bear on the reality of Muslim history as much as on the reality of Muslim societies today. A genuine effort was made to come to grips with the historical rupture that characterises the evolution of Muslim cultural development and, by better understanding it, learn to transcend it.[16]

4.3 On Method

The essence of the Award's enterprise is to develop a critical approach that expands the traditional confines of architectural criticism. This, although never fully articu-

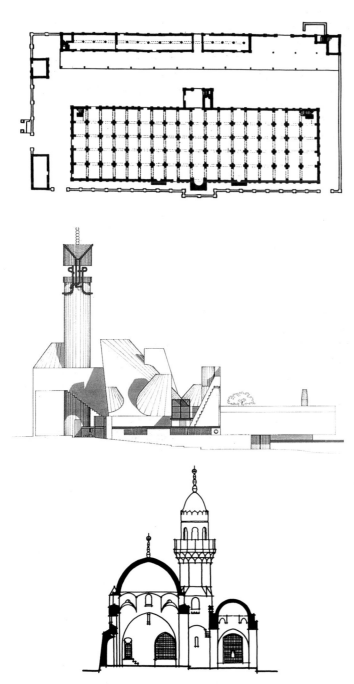

FROM ABOVE: AKAA, 1983, Great Mosque of Niono, Niono, Mali; AKAA, 1983, Sherefudin Mosque, Visoko, Bosnia; AKAA, 1989, Corniche Mosque, Jeddah, Saudi Arabia

lated, except in some parts of the Award book, *Space for Freedom*, was nevertheless the guiding philosophy behind much of the Award's work. A full articulation of that philosophy requires developing a detailed understanding of the heritage of the past as well as of the reality of the present. This expanded criticism would view architecture from multiple levels:

(a) The building qua building: the simplest, most direct appreciation of the building's functional response and aesthetic qualities: volume, space, light, materials, colours, etc. The entire lexicon of studied architectural criticism is brought to bear on the building, taking it apart and putting it together again both in physical and experiential terms.

(b) The building in its physical context: harmony or discord, intentional or unintentional, can be either positive or negative. Its relation to the environment, both natural and man-made, can enhance or diminish the stature of the achievement.

(c) The building in its cultural context: its 'fit' and appropriateness in the context of a cultural heritage expressed through a legacy of already-built forms produced throughout the society's history.

(d) The building in its international context: the positioning of the creative act as a part of the international network of currents, styles, schools, and ideas, as well as the extent to which it contributes to the evolution of that debate, either by reinforcement or by innovation.

(e) The building in its own local/regional intellectual milieu: to what extent does it make a statement on the immediate level of the debate that presses upon the intelligentsia of the region? This is no mere reflection of the international context, although it could be. The local/regional intellectual milieu is more concerned with issues of an urgency and immediacy that are geographically circumscribed, despite the fact that they may have universal overtones.[17]

Applying this type of criticism to the key buildings being constructed in the Muslim world today would shed light on both its architectural and contemporary cultural scene. While this was being done in the Award's offices and in its screening work, it was not made accessible to the public at large. Notwithstanding this lack of dissemination, the Award's methodology was, as I stated elsewhere:

though scientific and systematic, it is far from the arid scholasticism of much academic research. It explores and revitalises the myths and images that nourish the creative imagination of contemporary artists and architects. It develops the iconography and enriches the symbols that punctuate their contemporary universe. Most importantly, it does so by grounding these expressions of culture in a deep and unhurried understanding of the essence of the culture in all its myriad manifestations, past and present.

We hope that the integrity of this approach will separate this search from the doomed attempts to escape a chaotic and unsettling present by a headlong flight into a romanticised past, or the equally short-sighted approach that equates modernity with wholesale importation of Western technology, aesthetics, and patterns of behaviour. The former is tantamount to a slow suicide, for no community can isolate itself from the present, no matter how unpleasant its realities are. The latter approach is an agonising negation of self and identity, since no society can exclude its past from the constituents of its contemporary reality'.[18]

Resolving the dichotomy between traditional and modern outlooks through the application of this more thoughtful approach to criticism was the Award's most notable contribution to the debates about architecture in the Muslim world, and arguably also a contribution to the international debates in architectural circles. In application, this enabled the Award to recognise and differentiate between several approaches to architectural design in the Muslim world, which could be labelled as the following:

1 The Popular Approach
2 The Traditionalist Approach
3 The Populist Approach
4 The Adaptive-Modern Approach
5 The Modernist Approach

Note that the first is entitled the 'Popular Approach'. It is the result of the manifestation of popular culture honed by tradition. It produces the vernacular architecture so admired by many sensitive artists.[19] The other four are the work of trained architects responding in different ways. The Traditionalist Approach is espoused by those who master the popular and traditional idiom and choose to work within its confines, but manage to elevate it by their artistry (for example, Hassan Fathy and Ramses Wissa Wassef). The Populist Approach copies popular taste, usually producing work of mediocre quality, frequently vulgar, and excused in the name of commercial success. The last two represent a conscious effort to work in, and with, the present. The Adaptive-Modernist tries to adapt the architectural vocabulary of the past to respond to contemporary needs, reflecting contemporary sensibilities. The Modernists go boldly forth into developing a new vocabulary, although it may be drawn in part from the reinterpretation of elements from the past.

4.4 Some Examples of Mosque Architecture

There are examples of each of these categories among the winners in the different cycles. It is perhaps easiest to analyse the manifestations of these five 'approaches' by reviewing some of the outstanding winners, with their different approaches to symbolic architecture:

(a) *The Popular (Vernacular) Approach.* The Yaama and Niono Mosques have the serene balance of the traditional. Both were winners of the Award in 1986 and 1983 respectively.[20] Their message is clear and understood by the community they serve, and there is no denying the authenticity they exude, even to the foreign visitor. The only jarring note appears when in one part of the Niono Mosque, the mason tried to insert the modern material of corrugated tile; which he himself came to see as incongruous. On receiving his prize in 1983 in Istanbul, he informed the attendees at the seminar that he wanted to rectify it because it did not 'fit well' with the product of traditional builders.

(b) *The Traditionalist Approach.* There are architects, trained and registered, who choose to work in either the vernacular or historically relevant traditional architectural language. They imbue their work with the self-discipline that the mastery of these conventions, techniques and proportions requires. The small mosque of Hassan Fathy at Gourna is an example.[21] The current work of El-Wakil in Saudi Arabia, including the Corniche Mosque in Jeddah, which was recognised by the Award, is another.[22]

(c) *The Populist Approach.* The exuberance and delight that characterise the mixture of crudeness and stylishness of the Bhong Mosque in Pakistan says much about the present semantic disorder.[23] It is successful with the people it serves, and raises key issues that architects must address fully if they are to do their share in re-symbolising the Muslim environment of today.

(d) *The Adaptive-Modern Approach.* The Saïd Naum Mosque demonstrates a serious effort to be both distinctly modern and yet echo the traditional vocabulary.[24]

(e) *The Modernist Approach.* The Sherefudin White Mosque of Visoko, Bosnia stands out as an attempt to truly break with the surrounding traditional Bosnian architecture, while providing a landmark building. This project, which is an example of the Modern movement, has the convincing distinction of having been commissioned and paid for by the users. The seven-year debate that preceded its construction, and the subsequent use the community makes of it, shows that one can get traditional communities to sponsor avant-garde works and identify with them.

There are many issues in approaching the problems of designing a mosque for a contemporary Muslim community. The continuity of key symbolic elements (minaret, dome, gateway and mihrab) can be transformed without being degraded and can be retained while void of content. It is the skill of the architects, the depth of their understanding, and their affinity with the communities concerned, that makes the difference between kitsch and creativity. The Aga Khan Award winners have shown that creativity can have multiple manifestations, but that each must be authentic and true in order to be effective. There are many ways of providing better mosques and areas of congregation that respond to the need of Muslim societies, to anchor their self-identity into structures built today that speak to them and their children as eloquently as the symbols of the past did to their parents and grandparents. Only by freeing the imagination and creativity of archi-

AKAA, 1986, interior of the Bhong Mosque, Bhong Rahim Yar Khan, Pakistan

tects will this type of architecture make its all-important contribution to an integrated and integrating contemporary Muslim culture.

5. From Architecture to Intellectual Discourse

The debate on contemporary architectural expression in the Muslim world, like the broader intellectual debate of which it is also a part, can be summarised by two polar positions, while recognising a continuum of grey areas in between. At one extreme there is an Internationalist-Modernist position, which advocates high-tech architectural solutions because they represent 'the best of the West', frequently without regard to the suitability of these solutions to the physical and social environment. Flagrant examples of this approach abound.

At the other extreme, there are those who advocate an almost romantic attachment to the built forms of the past, not as examples of a particular historic period, but as the only real, authentic manifestation of a culture. These advocates are usually the same individuals who have been exceptionally concerned with the problems that could arise from 'opening up' the intellectual discourse between a Muslim/regional culture and an international, mostly Western, culture.

Emerging from the pursuit of this straitjacketed vision of authenticity has been a whole array of superficial manifestations of cultural bows in architectural expression. Elements of an established architectural vocabulary (such as arches, domes or gateways) are considered essential to ensure authenticity. There is no doubt that elements of the established architectural vocabulary, skilfully used and consistently reinterpreted, are an important dimension of producing culturally authentic architectural creations. It is equally true that there are many cheap attempts at 'Islamising' Western architecture by relying on these as superficial substitutes for a true effort at interaction with the milieu, its historical legacy, its cultural heritage, and its contemporary problems.

Great regional architects such as Rifat Chadirji have understood this point extremely well.[25] His emphasis on the abstraction of traditional form and reinterpretation in a modern context is, to this writer, the essential element for a positive growth of the contemporary culture of Muslim societies. This is a particularly important issue to highlight in view of the strong xenophobic currents that seek authenticity in romanticising the past and fleeing from the future. Such movements refuse to recognise the great burden incumbent upon contemporary architects in the Muslim world generally and in the Arab world specifically, where the pace of modernisation has been unprecedented in the annals of human history.

This extremely rapid modernisation has led to a critical loss of identity among many of the ruling socio-economic élites, whose influence in turn has led to total adoption of Western models, or to kitsch, or to a resurgence of the popularised vernacular. Worse, in many cases, the confrontation of élite perceptions of aesthetics and mass manifestations of popular taste have become ideologically charged. Elitism is confronted by populism. The latter, however, is a degraded form of the popular – a set of ideological concepts that are increasingly politicised in terms that reflect the cultural disintegration and uprooting found in contemporary Muslim societies. It is this phenomenon that intellectuals such as Arkoun have so cogently identified: an accelerated disintegration of the traditional semiotic frameworks in developing countries generally, and the Muslim world specifically.[26]

This explosive reality requires a special understanding of the manner in which traditional symbols have degenerated into signs and signals and, accordingly, in Arkoun's phrase, 'an intellectual commitment to re-symbolise the culture of today'.

The manifestations of this cultural situation also include another significant front: the advancing insertion of a modern, rapidly-changing technology into everyday lives traditionally governed by other concerns. The suitability of the technology, its adaptation to the needs of the population, and the social context are only one aspect of the issue. This is the part that has usually concerned architectural critics when looking at buildings. For both building as process and building as product, the technology issue has invariably been addressed in terms of suitability and adaptation to context. In more sophisticated analyses, the intrusion of technology into aesthetic precepts and norms has also been addressed. But the present discussion would add that technology with its various facets and dimensions involves a rationalist ordered universe, whose frame of reference is governed by a reductionist logic. That, in turn, confronts a manifest reality of semantic disorder due to the disintegration of semiotic frameworks referred to above. This confrontation finds its constructive resolution when the rationalist logic is utilised to provide the basis for a new set of conditions enabling the emergence of a new set of cultural symbols – much as the Modern movement in international (Western and Japanese) architecture came into being – thus liberating and broadening the horizons of an authentic, yet contemporary cultural response within the various regions of the Muslim world. Clearly, this type of interpretation of the creative acts of contemporary architects in the Muslim world involves a change in the perceptions of many architects, critics, clients, and more generally, the intelligentsia of the Muslim world.

This broadened domain, which would undoubtedly enhance the quality of the intellectual discourse around issues of relevance to the architectural profession, cannot remain divorced from the content and practice of architecture.

That, of course, is the essence of the intellectual contribution of the Award's seminars and publications as

FROM ABOVE: AKAA, Honourable Mention, 1980, Kampung Kebalen Surabaya Improvement Programme; AKAA, 1989, Grameen Bank Housing Programme, Bangladesh; AKAA, Honourable Mention, 1980, Kampung Kebalen Surabaya Improvement Programme

well as the winners. It is precisely because it is a broadening of the intellectual domain of the practice of architecture and architectural criticism that it has been controversial, and frequently misunderstood. But the controversy that the winners have generated attests to their ability to engage thinking architects intellectually, as well as visually. That, in the final analysis, is the highest compliment that can be paid to a creative work of art.

6. Future Directions

The preceding sections of this essay have described the intellectual journey of the Award over its first five cycles. While much terrain has been covered, and the hallmarks of the Award's approach are now well known, much still remains to be done to deepen the theoretical foundations of the critical method behind the approach, and much remains to be done to make that known to the outside world. Indirectly, the preceding discussion has also laid out an 'Agenda for Intellectual Action' and marked out the broad outlines of the 'space for freedom' approach that the Award advocates to promote rational discourse and sensitive criticism. Much more needs to be done to lay the foundations for such an expanded architectural criticism. Among the areas needing further discussion I will sketch out three:

1 The meaning of regionalism
2 The relevance of Post-Modern thinking
3 The need for a more gender-sensitive architectural criticism

The first can be dealt with more briefly because it is the subject of numerous treatises elsewhere.

6.1 On Regionalism

There is no question that regionalism, almost by definition, is a fundamental force in shaping good architecture in any given region of the world. The issues, however, are to balance the unique features of a properly regional expression with the broader concepts of the world-wide currents that we are all part of.[27]

Architects in the Muslim world have done outstanding critical work to analyse actual building to exemplify the best that regionalism has to offer. Works of Rifat Chadirji in Iraq and Ken Yaeng in Malaysia, for example, show thoughtful efforts to grapple with such issues.[28]

6.2 On Post-Modernism

The idea of 'Post-Modernism' in architecture was developed to express a whole range of responses that occurred in Western architecture after 1960. These were responses to the increasingly exhausted language of the formal geometries of the orthodox modern school. Applied on a large scale, had 'the white walls, the elegant framework of steel and glass, the loosely arranged ground plan, the transparency of the structure not become hopelessly exhausted and vapid?'[29]

Similar movements existed in all the arts, and the academics and art critics were all working at defining a theoretical and critical structure for Post-Modernism.[30] Sometimes they drew on philosophical work,[31] but mostly they worked within the domain of art criticism. In architecture, the pre-eminent supporter of Post-Modernism among the critics is undoubtedly Charles Jencks, whose body of writings provides the main theoretical foundation for the movement,[32] although the writings of eminent practitioners such as the late Charles Moore[33] and Robert Venturi[34] have contributed much to that effort. Jencks has defined Post-Modernism as:

> . . . double coding: the combination of Modern techniques with something else (usually traditional building) in order for architecture to communicate with the public and a concerned minority, usually other architects. The point of this double coding was itself double. Modern architecture had failed to remain credible partly because it didn't communicate effectively with its ultimate users – the main argument of my book *The Language of Post-Modern Architecture* – and partly because it didn't make effective links with the city and history. Thus the solution I perceived and defined as Post-Modern: an architecture that was professionally based and popular as well as one that was based on new techniques and old patterns. Double coding to simplify means both élite/popular and new/old . . .[35]

This is obviously an attractive idea. But there are profound dangers, as Jencks himself points out:

> The challenge for a Post-Modern . . . is to choose and combine traditions selectively . . . those aspects from the past and present which appear most relevant for the job at hand. The resultant creation, if successful, will be a striking synthesis of traditions; if unsuccessful, a smorgasbord. Between inventive combination and confused parody the Post-Modernist sails, often getting lost and coming to grief, but occasionally realising the great promise of a plural culture with its many freedoms.[36]

Aside from the talent of gifted individuals, is there something that would help avoid the catastrophes and increase the chances for brilliant works that engage the mind and the emotions of viewers while being responsive to their functional needs? Yes. Architects practising in the Muslim world need to have a much more profound understanding of the relevance of the past. Without such understanding, the choices they make in their designs – unless guided by exceptional intuition or luck – will probably lead to the 'confused parodies' mentioned by Jencks. Academics, researchers and critics must all do their share to lay the proper foundation for the training of architects and the education of the public. These are important conditions if one hopes to use 'double coding' and avoid 'confused parodies'. Such work must be grounded on a highly complete understanding of the past and an equally-shared vision between the artist and the viewers/users. These conditions are far from the contemporary reality of the Muslim world today. Indeed, some would doubt that even in the West such conditions exist, and there are serious questions being raised by Western critics.[37] The Award's work in this area could become an invaluable asset in the creation of the conditions in which such a discourse could take place, laying the foundations for an effective enrichment and transformation of the architectural vocabulary of the various regions of the Muslim world.

6.3 For a Gender-Sensitive Architectural Criticism

Lack of attention to the needs of any particular group is usually made more easy by the invisible nature of its presumed requirements.[38] Thus, until recent years when the architectural profession took to heart the needs of the handicapped, there was nothing wrong in the eyes of most designers or critics, to design public buildings without ramps for wheelchairs or with doorways that were too small to let them pass through, or to have elevators without braille buttons or sound signals for indicating the movement between floors. That this was an architecture that created and organised spaces which would inherently limit the accessibility of a public building for some members of the public, was not sufficiently appreciated. In fact, against this criterion some of the great buildings of this century (such as the Barcelona Pavilion of 1927) would be found lacking.

Similarly, the special needs of women and the unique contributions they bring to any society, *a fortiori* a Muslim society, are not sufficiently appreciated to provoke a more gender-sensitive architectural criticism. It is to the Award's credit that it tackled this issue in the seminar held in Indonesia on the 'Expressions of Islam in Buildings' in 1990. The discussion at that seminar has shown how women's special contributions are reflected in endless ways in today's rich canvas of Muslim societies in transition. The unique dilemma of the search for cultural identity in Muslim societies whose innate genius wants to make a contribution that risks being stifled and trampled by an overpowering and insensitive Western mass-consumption culture, finds an echo in microcosm in the dilemma of the contemporary Muslim woman trying to define her role and contribution in a society which frequently tries to suppress her contribution as a means of asserting its own individuality, its otherness from the dominant West. This oppressive atavism is neither inherently Islamic nor is it necessarily the sole or correct reading of the tradition of the past. Much less will it be the correct path for the future of truly Muslim societies.

This is not an appeal for Muslim scholars to adopt the ideological constructs or positions of Western feminism generally, or of Western feminist art criticism specifically.[39] Rather, it is an appeal to broaden our own architectural

AKAA, 1992, Demir Holiday Village, Bodrum, Turkey

AKAA, 1983, Darb Qirmiz Quarter, Cairo, Egypt

AKAA, 1980, Rustëm Pasa Caravanserai, Erdine, Turkey

criticism which has already made its own contribution in recognising the profound problems of cultural continuity and authenticity, as important elements to assert in the face of a 'historical rupture' that has rended the cultural fabric of Muslim societies. It is now pertinent to expand our concerns further and recognise the needs of women as well as their unique contributions to building society and buildings in a Muslim world in the throes of rapid change. Such a gender-sensitive architectural criticism would have certain characteristics.

The key to significant gender-sensitive architectural criticism is to transcend the mere recognition that women architects and women artists exist and to give them due recognition, which hitherto has been lacking. In other words, it should not just be the same old criticism with women added. What is required is to go to the heart of the thinking governing much of the present critical thinking in art and architecture, and to 'question the universal validity of those very myths and values and cultural assumptions that, in the past, have automatically excluded from the domain of Art the experiences of half of our population'.[40] Or as Carol Duncan pointed out, 'The value of established art thinking and how it functions as ideology must be critically analysed, not promoted anew'.[41]

6.4 Envoi

This brings us to the heart of the subject. Architectural criticism in Muslim societies has seldom been as ideologically charged as it is when discussing the presumed dichotomy of Modernity and Tradition. Some would restrict the allowable architectural vocabulary to a few traditional elements. Others would insist that only Muslims can build mosques (an historically inaccurate statement) and discussion of the subject tends to become so ideologically charged that dialogue, so essential to expand knowledge, is severely constrained.

In bringing to the fore the need for a more thoughtful criticism generally and, further, to develop gender-sensitive architectural criticism, we underline the need to bring to bear the modern tools of critical analysis, to deconstruct the discipline of architectural criticism itself,[42] so as to rebuild it anew, informed and enlightened by the process of critical deconstruction itself. To rebuild it with new insight that will not just be beneficial to establishing a place for women in Muslim art and architecture, not just to liberate their expressive and talented contributions as women, but to transcend feminism and through this rethinking of architectural criticism itself, to make a contribution to liberating the evolving cultures of Muslim societies. To liberate these cultures from insisting on defining themselves in negative terms of how they must be different from the rejected (Western) 'Other', to a new position where they can define themselves in the positive terms of their own achievements and fulfilment. This change in mental outlook is essential because it is by their thinking processes that Muslims everywhere are inventing the future in the crucible of their minds.

7. Conclusions

From the preceding discussion it becomes clear that the two sets of issues that have forced the Award to broaden both its scope and its coverage were inescapable if the Award wanted to be relevant to the reality of the Muslim world today. It needed to address the key to the definition of one's identity in a period of rapid change. It needed to address the social questions of a world that groans under the yoke of unbearable poverty. It needed to address the need for a new contemporary language that re-symbolises the environment of the coming generations of Muslims giving them a new language and articulating their evolving identity. Thus, the tripartite definition of the scope of its mandate is an adequate response to this complex reality. Equally, the tremendous variety and heterogeneity of the Muslim world made the limitation of the coverage of the Award to a few prizes difficult, if the selected examples were to carry a meaningful resonance of the complex and variegated realities reflected in the architecture of the Muslim societies of today.

Of particular relevance is the successful manner in which the Award has addressed all the key issues facing the built environment of the Muslim world. In addition, the Award has delineated the role of the architect in new and effective ways, for in a developing society, the architect with a social conscience is as much a necessity as the architect with an artistic consciousness.

Perhaps in the final analysis, it is the humility and tolerance of the Award, coupled with its unwavering commitment to excellence, that sets it apart from the many other efforts in the Muslim world today; humility in its willingness to define the endeavour as a search – that is the most enriching way to approach such a challenging task as the architecture of as diverse a set of people and societies as those that comprise the Muslim world today. To eschew the idea of a 'correct' solution to the problems of architecture in a rapidly changing world is the essence of opening up avenues for the talents of today and tomorrow, in order to forge a new and enriched identity for their communities.

Tolerance insofar as the Award did not exclude one set of solutions be it the Modernist or the Traditional for example, from the range of options that talented people can adopt and be recognised by the Award. It is a recognition of the reality that talented people can produce works of excellence and sensitivity, that definitely enrich their environments using different vocabularies and idioms.

Compassion and a social consciousness is reflected in the many awards given to works of social merit but lacking in visual appeal, such as the Kampung Improvement Programmes, the Grameen Housing Programme and other community-based schemes. In a world where the majority of the people live in abject poverty, this important new dimension in the recognition of architectural excellence was revolutionary and had a profound impact. It legitimated the work of many who wished to address the needs of the poor and the destitute, and gave recognition to their efforts – efforts which often go unnoticed and unappreciated, while honours and rewards are heaped upon those architects who take the large commissions for the wealthy individual and/or institutional clients.

By recognising building as a complex partnership that involves the client as much as the architect, the builder and the users, it set a new standard of recognition in the realm of architecture.

A concern with identity and the protection of the heritage is not only evident in the recognition of the sometimes heroic efforts of those who protect the heritage against the almost unstoppable pressures of urban transformation and natural decay. The passing on to future generations of this legacy is a welcome contribution that deserves recognition, subject to the same stringent standards of excellence that are applied to the selection of winners in the more generally accepted forms of architectural design expression. Indeed, it was also a recognition of the importance of retaining the past as an integral part of the present and the future, to enable the creation of a new architectural language, as in the words of TS Eliot:

Every phrase and sentence is right
When every word is at home
Taking its place to support the others
The word neither diffident nor ostentatious

An easy commerce of the old and the new
The common word exact without vulgarity
The formal word precise but not pedantic
The complete consort dancing together

Every phrase and every sentence
is an end and a beginning . . . [43]

Notes

1 For a detailed description of this momentous enterprise up to 1986, see Ismail Serageldin, *Space for Freedom: The Search for Architectural Excellence in Muslim Societies,* The Aga Khan Award for Architecture and Butterworth Architecture, Part I, London, 1989. For a detailed update to 1989 see Serageldin, *Al-Tajdid wal Ta'sil fi 'Imarat Al-Muitam'at Al-Islamiyya: Dirasa li Tajribat Ja'izat Al-Aga Khan Lil'Imara (Innovation and Authenticity in the Architecture of Muslim Societies: A Study of the Experience of the Aga Khan Award for Architecture),* The Aga Khan Award for Architecture, Part I, Geneva, 1989. For an update to 1992, see James Steele, 'Continuity, Relevance and Change: The Fifth Cycle of the Aga Khan Award for Architecture', in James Steele, ed, *Architecture for a Changing World,* The Aga Khan Award for Architecture and

AKAA, 1983, Great Mosque of Niono, Niono, Mali

Academy Editions, London, 1992, pp14-35.

2 For a discussion of these phenomena, see, among others, Ismail Serageldin, 'Mirror and Windows', *Litterae, The Review of the European Academy of Sciences and Arts 3* (23), 1993, Part 1, pp4-15.

3 AKAA archives, August 8, 1983, memorandum by Ismail Serageldin; the 1985 draft brief for the Master Jury by Ismail Serageldin, part of which appeared in *Space for Freedom*, Ismail Serageldin, pp274-77; and the full brief for the 1989 Jury, which appeared in *Al-Tajdid wal Ta'sil fi 'Imarat Al-Muitam' at Al-Islamiyya: Dirasa li Tajribat Ja'izat Al-Aga Khan Lil'Imara (Innovation and Authenticity in the Architecture of Muslim Societies: A Study of the Experience of the Aga Khan Award for Architecture)*, Ismail Serageldin, pp143-55.

4 Cairo Award Ceremony Address by His Highness The Aga Khan (Geneva: 1989).

5 For an indication of the seriousness of the Aga Khan Awards' intellectual efforts, see the vast array of publications issued by the Award. The efforts of just one cycle (1983-1986) are only partly captured in 'A Rising Edifice: Contributions Towards a Better Understanding of Architectural Excellence in the Muslim World', *Space for Freedom*, Part Three, Ismail Serageldin, pp208-95.

6 The Master Jury issues citations for each winning project and releases a short report at the time the prizes are awarded. These are the statements most frequently cited by the press.

7 Ismail Serageldin memo to the Steering Committee dated July 5, 1986, partly reprinted under 'Agenda for the Future', *Space for Freedom*, Ismail Serageldin, pp59-63.

8 AKAA, *Architectural Criticism*, The Aga Khan Award for Architecture, 1988.

9 AKAA, *Expressions of Islam in Buildings: Exploring Architecture in Islamic Cultures (Proceedings of an international Seminar)*, The Aga Khan Trust for Culture on behalf of The Aga Khan Award for Architecture, Geneva, 1991.

10 See Suha Özkan, 'A Pluralist Alternative', *Architecture for A Changing World*, ed James Steele, pp36-39.

11 Ismail Serageldin and Said Zulficar, 'A Living Legacy', *Space for Freedom*, Ismail Serageldin, pp250-53.

12 'Plus Ça Change', *A View from the Campidoglio*, Robert Venturi and Denise Scott Brown, Icon Editions, Harper Row, New York, 1984, p115.

13 'A Summation: Cultural Continuity and Cultural Authenticity', *Space for Freedom*, Ismail Serageldin, pp57-58, *et seq*, from which the following paragraphs are taken almost verbatim.

14 Ismail Serageldin, 'Faith and the Environment', *Space for Freedom*, pp213-25.

15 Oleg Grabar, 'From Utopia to Paradigm', *MIMAR* 18, 1985, pp41-45.

16 Mohammed Arkoun, 'Current Islam Faces Its Tradition', *The Aga Khan Award for Architecture, Architectural Education in the Islamic World*, Concept Media, Singapore, 1986, pp 92-103.

17 Ismail Serageldin, *Space for Freedom*, pp59-63.

18 Ismail Serageldin, *Space for Freedom*, p57.

19 Bernard Rudofsky, *Architecture without Architects*, Doubleday, New York, 1964; and Rudofsky, *The Prodigious Builder*, Harcourt Brace Jovanovich, New York, 1977.

20 For a presentation of the Niono Mosque refer to S Cantacuzino, ed, *Architecture in Continuity*, pp146-53; and for the Yaama Mosque refer to Ismail Serageldin, *Space for Freedom*, pp132-43.

21 JM Richards, I Serageldin, and D Rastorfer, *Hassan Fathy*, Mimar Books, Singapore, 1985, pp110-13.

22 The Corniche Mosque in Jeddah is described in Ismail Serageldin, *Al-Tajdid Wal Ta'sil fi' Imarat al-Mujtama' at Al-Islamiyya (Innovation and Authenticity in the Architecture of Muslim Societies)*, pp118-21.

23 For a discussion of the debates surrounding the Bhong Mosque see, among others, *MIMAR* 22, 1986; Ismail Serageldin, *Space for Freedom*, pp44-47 and pp144-54; and AKAA, *Criticism in Architecture (Exploring Architecture in Islamic Cultures 3)*, Concept Media Pte Ltd for The Aga Khan Award for Architecture, Singapore, 1989, pp16-35.

24 Ismail Serageldin, *Space for Freedom*, pp180-87.

25 Rifat Chadirji, *Concepts and Influences*, Routledge and Kegan Paul, London, 1987.

26 The concept of semantic disorder has received increasing attention in recent years. The advances in the applications of semiotics to other domains combined with the structuralist efforts at understanding change and development in societies (popular in the late 1960s and 70s) have now been challenged by the work of the post-structuralists, especially Michel Foucault and Jacques Derrida. Many, however, are concerned that much of the 'deconstructionist' viewpoint of individuals such as Derrida (which was very much in vogue in France in the late 70s and gained some adherents in the United States in the late 80s) is largely a form of inverted metaphysics of its own that precludes systematic recourse to evidence. The subject is broad, rich and quite complex. A good overview article is Frederick Crews's, 'In the Big House of Theory', *The New York Review of Books*, May 29, 1986, pp36-42.

27 See, among others, AKAA, *Regionalism in Architecture* (AKAA Series, *Exploring Architecture in Islamic Cultures 2*), 1985. See especially the essays by Suha Özkan, pp8-16; and BV Doshi, pp87-91

28 Ken Yaeng, *Tropical Urban Regionalism*, MIMAR Books/ Concept Media, Singapore, 1987.

29 Heinrich Klotz, *The History of Postmodern Architecture* (trans Radka Donnell), The MIT Press, Cambridge, Mass, 1988, (originally published in German, 1984).

30 See, among others, *The Idea of the Post-Modern: Who Is Teaching It?*, Essays by L Alloway, DB Kuspit, M Rosler, and J Van der Mack, Henry Art Gallery, University of Washington, Seattle, 1981.

31 See, among others, Jean-Francois Lyotard, *La Condition Postmoderne*, Les Editions de Minuit, Paris, 1979.

32 Among his many works on the subject, one of the most extensive treatments is Charles Jencks's, *The Language of Post-Modern Architecture*, 4th ed, Rizzoli, New York, 1977 and 1984.

33 See, for example, Charles Moore and Kent Bloomer, *Body, Memory and Architecture*, Yale University Press, New Haven and London, 1977.

34 See especially Robert Venturi's classic, *Complexity and Contradiction in Architecture*, The Museum of Modern Art, New York, 1966, which, to this writer, is vastly superior to his later writings.

35 See Charles Jencks, *What Is Post-Modernism?*, 2nd ed, Academy Editions/St Martin's Press, New York, 1987, p14.

36 *op cit*, p7.

37 See William Curtis, 'The Uses and Abuses of History', *Architecture Review*, August 1984.

38 This section is taken verbatim from Afaf Mahfouz and Ismail Serageldin, 'Women and Space in Muslim Societies', in AKAA, *Expressions of Islam in Buildings*, pp79-96.

39 For an excellent survey article of the subject, the reader is referred to Thalia Gouma-Peterson and Patricia Mathews, 'The Feminist Critique of Art History', *The Art Bulletin* (published by the College Art Association of America), LXIX (3), Sept 1987, pp 326-57. See especially sections IV and V, pp346-57.
Showing that there are no monolithic views on the subject, that excellent survey article was poorly reviewed by Cassandra Langer, 'Feminist Art History: Critique Critiqued', in *Women Artist News* 12 (5-6), Fall/Winter, 1987.
For a scholarly compendium of essays, see the anthology of American work given in Norma Broude and Mary Garrard, ed, *Feminism and Art History: Questioning the Litany*, Harper & Row, New York, 1982.
For a review of significant recent works, see Ellen Handy, 'Women, Art, Feminism', *Arts Magazine*, May 1989, pp25-31.

40 Norma Broude, 'Review of Germaine Greer's Obstacle Race, Munro's Originals and Loeb's Feminist Collage', *Art Journal*, XLI, 1981, p182.

41 Carol Duncan, 'When Greatness Is a Box of Wheaties', *Art Forum*, October 1975, p64.

42 For such a consistently radical position on methodology, albeit from a narrow Western feminist perspective, refer to Griselda Pollock, 'Women, Art, and Ideology: Questions for Feminist Art Historians', *Women's Art Journal*, Spring/Summer 1983, pp42-44.

43 TS Eliot, *Four Quartets*.

THINKING ARCHITECTURE

Mohamed Arkoun

When the Aga Khan created the Award for Architecture in 1978, Muslim societies were all engaged in a struggle for advancement and national unity, with references to two competing, opposing models: the Socialist-Communist model supported by the Soviet Union, and the Capitalist Liberal model defended by the United States and Western Europe. The Cold War between the two superpowers was reflected throughout the entire Third World, to which almost all so-called Muslim societies belong.

At the same time, the claim of nationalism by these Muslim societies and their desire for emancipation from 'Western' models was a central theme of all official discourse in Third World societies. In Arab countries, nationalism was as strong and recurrent an issue as the impetus for economic development which followed the patterns of the West they were rejecting ideologically. It was then difficult, if not impossible, to deal with any political, economic, social or cultural issue without immediately becoming enmeshed in ideological issues represented by the two superpower protagonists.

The idea of viewing contemporary issues in the Muslim world through architecture was highly attractive to those who expressed the need to be free of ideological frameworks imposed from those outside the Muslim world. Their desire was to create an open, new space for efficient inquiry wherein a rich exchange of ideas, concepts and solutions could take place under a multi-disciplinary approach. In this way, an accumulation of complex issues in each Muslim society dating back to the 50s and 60s could be examined and, hopefully, addressed.

During the first seminar organised in Aiglemont, France by the Aga Khan Award for Architecture, individuals such as Seyyed Hossein Nasr and Dogan Koban could not avoid stereotyping the authenticity and traditional revival on one side (Nasr) and the secularised models of modernity on the other (Koban). Hence, there has been no one single voice to plea for a radical criticism of both attitudes, showing their purely emotional, subjective basis, as exemplified today when the West speaks on 'fundamentalism' and fundamentalists reject the 'materialist', 'atheist', imperialist West.

From the beginning, apart from this ideological opposition, there has been a theoretical issue which architects and historians have had to face again and again: is there an *Islamic* architecture? If the answer is 'yes', how does one go about recognising and differentiating it from other types of architecture? What kind of criteria should be used for such a differentiation, so that architects, historians and art critics can produce types of architecture that would be able to meet the myriad of concerns expressed by nationalist forces to illustrate the Islamic personality claimed by so many people and states? More generally speaking, is it acceptable to historians and art critics to speak of Islamic arts at all? Would it not be more appropriate to speak of artistic activities within Islamic contexts instead?

I have had the privilege of being a member on four succeeding steering committees of the Aga Khan Award for Architecture from 1981 to 1992. I shared fascinating disputes with most famous architects like Charles Correa, Charles Moore, Bill Porter and John de Monchaux; and historians such as Oleg Grabar, Sherban Cantacuzino, Ronald Lewcock and Ismail Serageldin. Together we have created an exceptional circle of thinkers and researchers who meet regularly and operate in what I call a space of freedom for providing more freedom.

I personally kept developing, defending and illustrating a whole strategy to *rethink*, in modern perspectives, the totality of Islamic legacy through the issues raised by architecture and urbanism in contemporary Muslim societies. Serageldin and Grabar fully supported my determination to begin with architecture in search of deeper understanding and the more relevant answers which are needed in all domains of life, expression and development in Muslim societies.

What does this mean exactly? How does the strategy which was developed and which became the philosophy underlying the main trends of the Award activity and discourse become an ever-widening, flexible, integrative philosophy, the basis on which hundreds of building projects submitted each cycle will be evaluated by master juries, including the most praised architects in the world? I can summarise my own contribution to this vision under three interrelated directions for thought and action:

1   Architecture as a totalising activity.
2   Demands, expectations and answers in Muslim societies (*Waiting in the Future for the Past to Come*, a recent novel by Sabiia Khemiz).

Mosque at New Gourna, Egypt; PREVIOUS PAGE: 1986 Chairman's Award, Rifat Chadirji

3   Knowledge, thought and action.

I developed these themes and principles as I dealt with many topics in several essays published in the Award series:

Architecture as a totalising activity. I first had to learn how to communicate with architects who are used to expressing themselves with slides which show concrete spaces, volumes, forms and designs; while I, as an historian of Islamic thought, work only with 'abstract' concepts. Although architects do speak in terms of symbols, metaphors, mythical visions and aesthetic expressions, they do not extend these concepts with a comparative analysis of the definitions proposed for it by philosophers, anthropologists, psychologists and sociologists. They refer also to the cultural past, the identities claimed by nations, social groups and communities, but they do not consider how each identity is articulated through historical processes, combining religion, politics, layers of beliefs, rituals and complex collective memories.

It has been easy to show that all these references have not been integrated in the same strategy of thinking rooted in the established programme of teaching which can be translated into architectural discourse. Architects trained in the Western tradition of Beaux Arts, acquainted with the debates on Classicism and Modernism since Bauhaus and Le Corbusier, have been asked to build huge projects like banks, hotels, official palaces and mosques in societies where the search for Islamic identities became vital during the 1960s, 70s and 80s. Apart from those 'natives' who have been trained at MIT, Paris, London and Berlin, very few – if any – have been encouraged to learn the fundamentals of Islamic culture and history. However, all share the same concern for restoring fragments of broken identities.

Muslim architects such as Hassan Fathy, Rifat Chadirji, Mohammed Mekiya, Fazlu-l-Rahman and Al-Wakil have contributed to the debate with buildings and theoretical views on Islamic architecture and urbanism. None of them had – or has – an overview on Islamic thought in its historical and intellectual dimensions, to impose an evolving modern style based on a critical reassessment of Islamic tradition. Al-Wakil has built many mosques to reaffirm the richness and solidarity of Islamic inspiration, but he does not integrate the devastating crisis of Islam as a religion, of societies where Islam is claimed as the historical model in opposition to Western hegemonic civilisation in the near future. The concept and substance of tradition are used more as a romantic device for self-validation needed by privileged 'élites' rather than a field of inquiry to recognise the reasons and forces which led Muslim societies to the present disintegration.

These observations do not represent attempts to criticise the works of leading architects, they are meant to point to the fundamental theoretical issue: is architecture an activity separated from other intellectual, artistic, cultural productions, or is it necessarily dependent on, or articulated to, these fields of creativity, innovation, critical evaluation, emancipation from alienation and wrong consciousness? In other words, how would one evaluate, from this point of view, the Ottoman Empire characterised by a rich, sumptuous architecture and a narrow, conservative, oppressive intellectual life?

I keep searching, confronting and thinking about this issue as it is illustrated today by many projects nominated for the Aga Khan Award for Architecture. Furthermore, intellectual life today is rather weak, controlled by the various states: cultural activities are limited in their inspiration and sociological expansion; while ideological themes and slogans are, on the contrary, overwhelmingly dominating. How does one evaluate architectural works in such a context?

Demands, expectations and answers in Muslim societies. Demands and expectations are on the scale of increasing demographic pressures. In several societies, the population has tripled in the thirty years from 1960, which means that seventy per cent of the people are under thirty-five. This simple fact should inspire new solutions, new scales, new designs in architecture. However, since the states are the principal clients for important projects, the rest of the citizens are either too poor or incorrectly motivated to impose the relevant answers to present needs upon the architects.

Stereotyped images of 'Islamic' culture are projected as being a part of architectural expression in both public and private buildings. At the same time, modern design as it is known and spread in Western societies, is unavoidable and shapes the 'built' environment everywhere. Traditional villages, cities and precious monuments related to different periods and cultures are doomed to deterioration and disintegration due to a lack of interest, resources and historical consciousness. They are located in those places which have been invaded by the rural population, who has up-rooted and disenfranchised itself, looking for precarious shelters, reduced to a *populist* way of life. Social housing is desperately irrelevant, or out of scale given the demographic pressures.

How can excellence in architecture as a fundamental right of architects to express themselves as creative artists be preserved in this context? We have forced this issue several times in the ongoing inquiry of the Award. Answers differ with the philosophical visions and political positions of architects, intellectuals, artists, writers and politicians. It is a fact, nevertheless, that excellence is more and more inconceivable, unreachable, or limited to private houses which cannot contribute to the education of a large public for claiming quality, beauty, comfort, and cultural values in the building environment.

Knowledge, thought and action. Architecture is required to link these three as a totalising activity. This cannot necessarily be reached without two major conditions: a multi-disciplinary training of architects while they are learning and practising; and special institutions to enhance a continuous communication between architects, urbanists and a large public – the potential clients – in each society. These two conditions are far from being fulfilled, especially for Muslim societies where the teaching of the Beaux Arts is new, recent and dominated by Western mores in all fields.

We once again face the weakness, or total absence of a scientific, critical, widespread teaching of Islamic thought and local cultures. I developed these points on several occasions, and in many cities throughout the Muslim world. However, it remains a difficult task to introduce a new curriculum, new programmes of education, and new articulations of fields of knowledge as suggested above. Even at MIT, the history of Islamic thought is not yet accepted as an organic part of the curriculum followed by the students. I am not pleading for the knowledge of Islam as a religion. On the contrary, I have always insisted on the necessity of developing a *critical* study of Islamic thought and local cultures, to enable architects and urbanists in their search for new answers to changing contexts and increasing demands. Only critical study can help to get rid of artificial, so-called Islamic identities, and to give free space for innovative creativity.

In aural cultures, each member of the group could participate fully in the culture through commonly-shared language and daily practices, without any need to go to school for such training. In our societies, which are based on the written transmission of cultures, schools are an institution which separates a learned élite from the rest of the populous who are deprived of official education and marginalised in their own aural culture. This situation holds true and is decisive in many Muslim societies. It explains how urgent the need is to adapt the official teachings of this anthropological segregation of two worlds of culture and existence which has perpetuated a strong system of inequities. To my knowledge, only Hassan Fathy approached this issue in his beautiful book, *Building with People.*

Interior of the dome, the mosque in New Gourna, Egypt

WRITING ON THE ARCHITECTURE OF ISLAM
THE LAST TWENTY YEARS

Mohammad Al-Asad

The conception and construction of works of architecture differs from the creation of an architectural tradition. The former is only a prerequisite for the realisation of the latter. An architectural tradition is only born when authors, whether architects, historians or critics, write about works of architecture as belonging to distinct taxonomic categories. Accordingly, although examples of the vast body of buildings now collectively identified under the heading of 'Islamic architecture' had been produced since the seventh century, it was not until the nineteenth century that this tradition was 'invented'.

One of the earliest works that identified architectural vocabularies as distinctly belonging to the Islamic world is a 1721 general history of architecture written by the Viennese architect Johann Bernhard Fischer von Erlach. He discusses what he refers to as Arab, Turkish and Persian architectural traditions, and includes illustrations of buildings from Istanbul, Mecca, Medina and Isfahan.[1] Publications providing more detailed information on the architecture of the various regions of the Islamic world began to appear in the late eighteenth century. During the 1780s, the British artist, William Hodges, published drawings on India's Islamic and Hindu architectural heritage. Two other British artists, Thomas Daniell and his nephew William, published their drawings of India's Islamic and Hindu architecture between 1795 and 1808.[2] The *Description de l'Egypte*, the twenty-three volume work devoted to Egypt's natural, ancient and Islamic history, included information on the architectural heritage of Islamic Egypt. *Description*, which was compiled by the French scholars who accompanied Napoleon during his expedition to Egypt between 1798 and 1801, and was published between 1809 and 1821, includes perspectives and measured drawings of a number of the country's Islamic monuments such as the mosque of Ibn Tulun and the madrasa of Sultan Hasan.

Other publications devoted to the Muslim architectural heritage of regions including al-Andalus, Egypt, Iran and Algeria, appeared during the following few decades. The authors of these publications were usually European architects with little or no knowledge of local languages and histories, and their publications were therefore of an amateurish nature. Nonetheless, these authors laid the foundations for studying the architectural heritage of the Islamic world.[3] Their writings did not deal with the Islamic world as a collective entity, but discussed each region separately, and it was not until the mid-nineteenth century that these regionally defined architectural traditions began to be grouped under all-embracing headings such as 'Islamic' or 'Muhammadan' architecture.[4]

A comprehensive understanding of an architectural tradition includes studying the evolution of the literature devoted to it. Such literature defines the characteristics constituting a given tradition, creates its sub-categories, and selects the monuments belonging to them. Although in its most rudimentary form the evolution of the discourse on the architectural heritage of the Islamic world can be traced back to the early eighteenth century, the last two decades have been the most eventful. The following pages will discuss some of the general themes that have characterised writings on this field since the 1970s.

Three important publications dealing with the architecture of the Islamic world appeared in 1973. Each of these different works has had a profound effect on the general understanding of this architectural heritage. They are *The Sense of Unity* by Nader Ardalan and Laley Bakhtiar, *Architecture for the Poor* by Hassan Fathy, and *The Formation of Islamic Art* by Oleg Grabar. Prestigious American university presses published all three books: the University of Chicago Press published the former two, whilst Yale University Press published the last. Beyond these similarities, however, the three works show considerable diversity in the educational and professional backgrounds of their authors, their subject matter and their methodological approaches.

The author of *The Formation of Islamic Art*, Oleg Grabar, is a leading authority in the field of Islamic art and architecture. He taught at the University of Michigan and at Harvard University, and is presently a professor at the Institute for Advanced Study in Princeton. As the title indicates, the book deals with the evolution of early Islamic art and architecture. A significant quality of this work lies in its departure from the descriptive and documentary approaches predominant in earlier writings on the field. *The Formation of Islamic Art* does not treat the art and architecture of Islam as isolated phenomena, but studies them within their cultural context. It addresses a number of fundamental issues such as defining the adjective 'Islamic' as it applies to art and architecture, and identifying the symbolic and formal changes that the arrival of Islam brought to the art and architecture of the lands in which it prevailed. In addition to strongly influencing students and specialists in the field of Islamic art and architecture, the book's breadth, interpretative nature and engaging manner has made it one of the few books on the field that non-specialists are likely to read.[5]

The author of *Architecture for the Poor*, the late Egyptian architect Hassan Fathy (1900-1989), is among the Islamic world's most acclaimed architects. Fathy is best known for the design and construction of the village of New Gourna in rural Egypt during the 1940s. He completed the village for relocated Egyptian villagers within the confines of a tight budget, and relied exclusively on the materials, building techniques and architectural forms prevalent in the vernacular architecture of rural Egypt. *Architecture for the Poor* primarily explained the experience of designing and constructing New Gourna, and was the primary medium through which Fathy communicated his ideas to an international audience. As a result of his accomplishments, Fathy became a role model, even a hero, for young architects to find inspiration. His work communicated a sense of social idealism and sensitivity to one's cultural heritage. He turned to what is viewed as the pure and uncorrupted vernacular architecture of the countryside for models, and avoided the abstraction and ahistoricism of Western twentieth-century modernism. At the same time, he used a representational and culturally-specific architectural vocabulary, but bypassed the vocabularies of the Islamic revival which European architects introduced to the Islamic world during the second half of the nineteenth century. Until very recently, many in the Islamic world associated the vocabularies of the Islamic revival with colonialism, national weakness and underdevelopment.

These two books represent the two main categories of writing on the architecture of the Islamic world that have prevailed since the 1970s. *The Formation of Islamic Art* provides a continuation, though with substantial modifications, of a scholarly tradition of historical writing on the pre-modern architecture of the Islamic world. In *Architecture for the Poor*, we see the emergence of a new and less widespread genre of writing in which practising architects from the Islamic world articulate their own experiences and opinions on contemporary architectural practice; as well as writing on its historical architectural heritage.

The Sense of Unity is an example of this overlap between the two categories of writings. Although one of the authors is a practising Iranian architect and the other has had training in architecture, the book addresses the pre-modern Islamic architecture of Iran rather than contemporary architecture. *The Sense of Unity* aims at investigating the spiritual dimension of that historical architectural tradition, and at exploring the esoteric

meanings behind its forms. The book, however, can be criticised for its lack of methodological scholarly rigour. Furthermore, the architecture of Islamic Iran is treated as a static and timeless phenomenon rather than the outcome of a process of continuous historical evolution.[6] Still, their emphasis on mysticism has appealed to architects practising in the Islamic world. To these architects, a publication such as *The Sense of Unity* asserts the unique individuality of the architecture of Islam in comparison to that of the West, and presents it as an architecture based on the spiritual rather than the material.

The appearance of these publications coincided with important economic and political developments that affected many parts of the Islamic world, such as the dramatic rise in oil prices connected to the 1973 Arab-Israeli war and the subsequent oil embargo which Arab oil-producing countries attempted to impose on a number of Western nations. The economies of numerous Islamic countries depend heavily on oil revenues. Most of the members of the Organisation of Petroleum Exporting Countries (OPEC) are Muslim countries. A number of non-oil exporting Muslim countries also rely on OPEC countries for their economic well-being, through a variety of economic ties connecting the two groups of nations. The sudden rise in oil prices in 1973 fuelled unprecedented construction booms in many parts of the Islamic world. These provided architects from both inside and outside the Islamic world with considerable opportunities to build and experiment. Much of the latter concentrated upon reviving notions of the Islamic world's architectural heritage. These developments have contributed strongly to the interest in Islamic architecture since the 70s.

One manifestation of this increased interest in the architecture of the Islamic world has been the founding of the Aga Khan Award for Architecture in 1976, and the Aga Khan Program for Islamic Architecture at Harvard University and the Massachusetts Institute of Technology in 1979. Both organisations have served a complementary set of roles. The Aga Khan Award has disseminated information concerning the architecture of the Islamic world, and has celebrated and rewarded excellence in contemporary architectural and urban design, and in historical restoration. It has also sponsored conferences and symposiums which have provided forums for architects, planners and historians to debate issues relating to the state of architecture in the Islamic world. The Aga Khan Program for Islamic Architecture has also sponsored conferences, symposiums and workshops, but more importantly, has trained a new generation of architectural historians and architects whose main area of interest is the Islamic world. For the purposes of this essay, the significance of these two institutions lies in their sponsorship of publications devoted to architecture. These have included proceedings of professional and scholarly gatherings, and monographs devoted to architecture and architectural history.

The Aga Khan Program for Islamic Architecture has also supported the publication of *Muqarnas*, a yearly periodical which first appeared in 1982, and which features scholarly articles on Islamic art and architecture. Other journals dealing with the same subject matter also appeared during the late 70s and early 80s. *Mimar*, a quarterly journal which first appeared in 1979, concentrated on the contemporary practice of architecture in the Islamic world.[7] Other Western language journals include *Arts and the Islamic World* and *Islamic Arts*, both of which have appeared since 1982. Although not devoted exclusively to the art and architecture of the Islamic world, the journal *AARP* (Art and Archaeology Research Papers), which appeared between 1976 and 1982, regularly featured articles in this field. The journal was continued under the title *Environmental Design: Journal of the Islamic Environmental Design Research Centre*, which appeared in 1984 and 1985. Journals published in the local languages of the Islamic world include *al-Benaa*, a Saudi Arabian, Arabic-language journal which first appeared in 1979, and which concentrates upon the contemporary practice of architecture and landscape architecture. These various publications have provided a forum for a continuous presentation and exchange of ideas concerning contemporary and historical architecture in the Islamic world.

The changes initiated in the 1970s provided momentum for developments that have taken place during the past decade. The rate of publishing works devoted to the architecture of the Islamic world has increased during this period. A number of publications have continued an early tradition concerned with basic documentation, for example, describing monuments with text, drawings, and photographs; reconstructing partially – or no longer surviving – monuments; and establishing dates of monuments and identities of patrons. Although such works have appeared since the nineteenth century, the need for them remains strong, since the documentation of the architectural production of the Islamic world is far from complete. An increasing number of publications has continued the methodological direction powerfully expressed in *The Formation of Islamic Art*, and have approached architectural production within the context of surrounding cultural conditions. At the same time, new frontiers are being explored, including the practice of architecture and the use of architectural drawings, models and manuals from the pre-modern Islamic world.[8]

Another very important development to have taken place during the past decade is the increased interest in studying the Islamic world's modern architectural past, ie the architecture of the nineteenth and twentieth centuries. Such architecture remained, until very recently, a rarely studied subject. The major books which survey Islamic architecture usually only examine monuments conceived before 1800.[9] Although the architecture conceived in the Islamic world during the modern period often lacks the originality and vitality of earlier examples, it nonetheless remains an integral part of that world's cultural heritage, and effectively expresses the powerful changes and ruptures that affected it during that period. The increasing tendency towards including the modern period within the boundaries of what we identify as Islamic architecture, will allow us to understand better an important phase of the Islamic world's architectural and overall cultural evolution. Furthermore, it will enable us to identify the missing links connecting the architecture of the pre-modern period with that of the present.

During the past decade, an increasing number of publications have attempted to articulate a methodological framework for studying the architectural production of the Islamic world. These works have come from both academicians and professional architects. Much of Oleg Grabar's work has partly aimed at formulating such a framework. His recently published *The Mediation of Ornament*, which explores the role of ornament in our perceptions and understandings of art and architecture, is a work belonging to the heading of art and architectural theory as much as to the field of Islamic art and architecture.[10] The Iraqi architect Rifat Chadirji has expressed the most rigorous explorations of architectural theory provided by a practising architect from the Islamic world. Chadirji, the second recipient of the Aga Khan Award for Architecture's Chairman Award (the first and only other recipient so far has been Hassan Fathy), has published three books on architecture, one in English and two in Arabic.[11] Chadirji approaches architectural form as the end product of a process of dialectic interaction between the social needs of a given society and the technologies available to it. He applies this methodological framework to explain the changes that have transformed architecture in both the industrialised and developing worlds during the modern period. He argues that changes in social needs and technology during the modern era have made traditional architectural forms and practices obsolete. He also argues that within the context of the developing world, the mastering of industrial and post-industrial technologies is a prerequisite for generating contemporary indigenous and viable architectural vocabularies.

More people from the Islamic world are writing on its architecture than before. The increased participation of these authors offers a number of positive developments. They supplement the field with a native knowledge of its languages. This skill, among other things, will increase the exploration of textual evidence relating to architecture. Although most of these scholars have been trained in Western institutions, they inject an element of diversity and introduce new perspectives for the study of a field that, until recently, was defined exclusively by Westerners, and therefore suffered from the biases often associated with studying the 'other'. The study of the past should, of course, never be the prerogative of those who

New Gourna, Egypt

claim it as theirs. Such a monopoly encourages ethno-centric and religiocentric interpretations that can easily degenerate into exercises in cultural self-gratification. Nonetheless, it is primarily through examining its own past that a group can define itself, understand the forces that have shaped it, articulate hopes, and formulate directions for the future.

In spite of these changes, the participation of the cultural and educational institutions of the Islamic world in the study of their architectural heritage in a rigorous and scholarly manner, remains limited. Most scholars of Islamic architecture from the Islamic world are affiliated with Western institutions. They primarily write in Western languages for Western audiences, with Western presses publishing their works. The use of a Western language such as English does make their writings accessible to an international audience since English has become the *lingua franca* both inside and outside the Islamic world. However, the use of English limits accessibility to readers within the Islamic world where not all have an adequate command of the language. Also, since Western presses usually publish Western language writings, most of these writings are too expensive for readers in the Islamic world. Another consequence of the phenomenon that

most scholars from the Islamic world write in Western languages, is that the vocabulary needed for the study of architectural history, theory and criticism remains to be adequately developed for most of the languages of the Islamic world.

Although most of the academic centres carrying out specialised research on the architecture of the Islamic world, and most of the publishing houses disseminating their results are located in the West, the field remains a relatively minor and underdeveloped subject of study there. Even the impressive progress achieved during the past two decades in the study of Islamic architecture has not removed it from its position of relative obscurity. Although advances will continue to be made, there are no indications that any significant changes will affect the study of the field in the West during the near future. The challenges of providing the study of Islamic architecture with the attention and support it deserves will therefore need to be met by the cultural institutions of the Islamic world itself. Unless these institutions substantially increase their commitment to the exploration of their architectural heritage, the field of inquiry identified as Islamic architecture will remain a minor field located at the margins of Western academic knowledge.

NOTES

1 Johann Bernhard Fischer von Erlach, *Entwurff einer historischen Architektur*, 1721.

2 William Hodges, *Select Views in India, Drawn on the Spot in the Years 1780, 1781, 1782 and 1783*, plates pub 1785-88; and Thomas and William Daniell, *Oriental Scenery*, six parts, 1795-1808.

3 These works include James Cavanah Murphy, *The Arabian Antiquities of Spain*, 1813; Pascal-Xavier Coste, *Architecture Arabe ou monuments du Kaire*, 1837-39; idem, *Monuments moderne de la Perse*, 1867; MA Delannoy, *Etudes artistique sur la Regence d'Alger*, 1835-37; and Jules Goury and Owen Jones, *Plans, Elevations, Sections and Details of the Alhambra*, two vols, 1842 and 1845.

4 Concerning the evolution of studying the architecture of the Islamic world during the nineteenth century, see Mohammad Al-Asad, 'The Re-invention of Tradition: Neo-Islamic Architecture in Cairo', *Proceedings of the 28th International Congress of the History of Art,* forthcoming.

5 Yale University Press published a revised edition of *The Formation of Islamic Art* in 1987. For a recent evaluation of the impact of this work on the study of Islamic art and architecture, see Robert Hillenbrand's review in *Oriental Art*, Spring 1989, pp46-47.

6 For a critical assessment of *The Sense of Unity*, see Gulru

Necipoglu, *Geometry and Decoration in Islamic Architecture (10th-16th Centuries): The Evidence of a Late Timurid Design Scroll*, Santa Monica, California: Getty Center for the History of Art and the Humanities, forthcoming.

7 *Mimar* unfortunately ceased publication in the summer of 1992. Hopefully, this will only be of a temporary nature.

8 *op cit*, Necipoglu.

9 This avoidance of monuments conceived after 1800 is evident in the two major comprehensive surveys of Islamic architecture in use today. See John Hoag, *Islamic Architecture*, revised edition, Rizzoli, 1987; and George Michell, ed, *Architecture of the Islamic World*, Thames and Hudson, London, 1978.

10 Oleg Grabar, *The Mediation of Ornament*, Princeton University Press, Princeton, New Jersey, 1992.

11 Rifat Chadirji's books on architecture which have been published so far are *Shari' Taha wa Hammersmith*, [Taha Street and Hammersmith], *Mu'assasat al-abhath al'arabiyya*, Beirut, 1985; *Concepts and Influences: Towards a Regionalized International Architecture*, Routledge & Keegan Paul, London, 1986; and *al-Ukhaydar wa'l Oasr al-Balluri* [al-Ukhaydar and the Crystal Palace], Riad al-Rayyes Books, London, 1991.

FROM ABOVE, L to R: AKAA, 1989, National Assembly Building, Dhaka, Bangladesh; AKAA, 1983, Residence Andalous, Sousse, Tunisia;
Interior of the New York Islamic Cultural Centre Mosque; AKAA, 1983, Residence Andalous, Sousse, Tunisia

THE TANGLED WEB OF TIME

Future of the Muslim Past and The Aga Khan Award for Architecture

S Gulzar Haider

Architecture dwells in time but happens at the twilight between past and present, and present and future. The architect is enchanted by the markings of time that have gone by. Through sensual experiences of real journeys, through the imagination as it swims through texts, through the reading of drawings and photographs, and through the gift of memory and pattern-seeking disposition, the architect constructs the past. Past is real in the sense that its evidence is scattered all around. It is structured cognition of what has already happened. To the architect, however, past is also an emotional disposition, like lingering sensations of a powerful dream whose end is not yet certain.

The architect is caught in the inner labyrinth of the happening time itself. He knows the present by being in it, by attending its birth at every catastrophic moment. He marks time by organising these exploding bits of happening time into events that make sense in his own world. Often these events are the buildings being constructed but sometimes they are demolitions, graftings, transplantations, refurbishings. He is, sometimes by choice, always by default, voting on the value of past as it seeks its relevance and continuity into the present. As a restorer he is a healer of time past. As a demolisher he is its executioner, a mercy killer in his own mind, convinced of the higher value of the 'new' that he proposes to substitute for the 'old'. In his manner of grappling with the present, the architect professes his personality.

It is as a designer, however, that the architect encounters time in its most awesome incarnation: the time yet to happen, the future. While the historian seeks structure, causality and continuity in a time that has already happened, the designer posits a complex reality in the as yet 'un-happened' time. But this future is an elusive concept, though everyone would claim to 'know' what it is. Is it a domain of limitless potentiality, the fruition of a heroic resolve, the manifest will, an unfolding destiny, or even a Divinely guaranteed prophecy? Or is it a calendar of events projected from accurate mathematical models of well-behaved continuous systems? Or is future itself a domain of design, a mouldable amorphous clay that awaits the hands of an inspired potter?

Architecture may be conceived and gestated as form and space but eventually it is culturally authenticated, symbolically charged, manifest time. It is visible because it is conscious, deliberated, wilful dissonance in the otherwise grand flow of terrestrial and cosmic time. Pyramids of Giza are architecture. A pyramidal geological outcrop in the desert, however 'authentic' in its silhouette, is not architecture. The former is a heroic attempt to dam the river of time, the latter is a mere exhibit of détente between various contending forces of physical nature. The Taj Mahal is architecture capturing time from the obliterating veil of death. It is also architecture conjecturing the Day of Judgement, the very end of time.

Time and its Pirates

We are all familiar with colonisation as the phenomena of displaced power, exploitative economics and bartered identities. The trader metamorphosed into soldier and eventually adorned himself with vice-regal plumes. The healer of bodies and the saviour of souls, in fact, was the kidnapper of minds, the soldier of fortune dressed as the ambassador of civilisation. Entire continents were diagnosed as 'dark' so that they could be 'enlightened'. Unlike the marauding conquerors of another era who demolished, looted and left, the coloniser worked as a pernicious parasite weaving tunnels of destruction and building new facades with the debris.

Much has been written by the loyal apologists of colonisation. They see it as an inevitable process of superior ideas of Europe, as the rays of a rising sun cutting through the mist of archaic beliefs and customs. Much has also been produced as a scream against the pirates of time, the kidnappers of mind, the stealers of soul and the polluters of morality. In the final analysis colonisation is manifest through its accumulated consequences and we are interested in what happened to the cultural, and specifically the architectural enterprise.

The fabric of time unravelled. The intimate interlacing of tradition, legend and myth, which shared a mutually necessary position in the temporal carpet stretching from here to eternity, loosened and ultimately became undone. The indigenous past became a condemned space where irrelevance reigned and archaic, unenlightened words and behaviours continued. It was quarantined as a site for the European historian, archaeologist, cartographer, painter and writer, the licensed voyeurs, the forensic scholars.

OPPOSITE: AKAA, 1992, Kairouan Conservation Programme, Kairouan, Tunisia; ABOVE: AKAA, 1980, National Museum, Doha, Qatar

Ultimately the past was pronounced dead. All its visual manifestations declared historical, its creative production rendered quaint, its texts removed, its languages degraded. The chamber where poets and scholars gathered around the patron became the setting for an 'English *sahib*' in uniform, strutting himself on a throne-like chair, watching the '*Nautch* Girls' whose entourage is seen pathetically spread around them on the floor. The experience though mutually dependent is definitely not shared. The *Nautch* is a show, the *Sahib* is the voyeur. The seductive display is the vanquished culture's only remaining offering, and the power of gaze, the conqueror's bounty. They share the same clinical moment in one hall but the two are in totally different times. The former are dancing their dark, condemned fate in a chamber of stale time, the latter sits in the commanding space of power at the helm of the future that it is his destiny to shape.

Shahjehanabad, the 'abode of the king of the world' resigned to its new title as 'Old' Delhi, accepted its destiny to fester in its own time swamp. 'New' Delhi became the manifest legitimisation of the British Raj. Architecture choreographed the imperial procession of coronation that elevated that distant place, India, to the Nirvanic stature of being the 'Jewel in the Crown'. New Delhi, the *Sahib*, Old Delhi, the *Nautch Girl*! The signs, symbols, languages, some mannerisms, dresses and even the architectural and decorative motifs of India were appropriated, not for their intrinsic value, but to achieve the affect that the New Emperor is benevolent and sensitive to the memories of the subjects. If Lutyens appropriated some Mughal vocabulary, it was the gracious gesture of the *Sahib* putting on the local ceremonial hat over his imperial demeanour in order to win the local hearts.

Golden Cage of the Colonised Time

Beyond the apparent sympathies imbedded in colonial architecture, and garden-like promenades supposedly emulating the Mughal gardens, something much more serious had happened. The 'native' had not only accepted the grand architectural scale, stark urban hierarchies and racial quartering, but had started to dream about inheriting it one day. The vanquished had become convinced of his lot and started to see a higher reason in the success of his conqueror. The hostage became his own ransom, fell in love with the kidnapper and thus rendered the protocol of imprisonment unnecessary. Macauley's plan had done more than create a class of 'interpreters between us and the millions whom we govern; a class of persons, Indian in blood and colour but English in taste, opinions, in morals and intellect'. It mutated a self-coloniser constantly battling his traditional alliances, forever burying his past, struggling to be alien in his own house. He denied his memories. He stopped painting miniatures. His *Haveli* turned inside out. He wished a colonial *Kothi*, no matter how small, no matter how distant, as long as it was in the orbits of the Connaught Place. Unlike Sidharta, who abandoned the gilded cage of his own palace to fly with Simurgh, this son of India willingly cut his own wings and became the loyal parrot of the Whitehall.

The theatre of colonial empire eventually folded up. But it left behind its architectural sets, cultural props and costumes of power. The local stage-hands who could best mimic the originals rushed onto the stage and started to improvise. What was profoundly Europeanised was superficially Indianised or Islamised as the new nation-state's declared identity demanded. The names of the streets changed; royal statues from New Delhi's Kings Way or Lahore's Charing Cross were taken to the parks or museums and in their place India decided to erect Mahatma Gandhi, and Pakistan placed an open stone Book on a seat. To the mutated self-coloniser, to the parrot in this golden cage of alien time, to the new stage manager carrying on the old theatre, it seemed only natural that Mahatma must stand where the British Emperor stood, artificially elevated in this colonial Versailles. And to the pious placers of the Book it was perhaps like a chess move: 'taking your Queen for our Book!' These architectural moves, innocent and well meaning as they might have been, are quite telling in that changes of signs and banal substitutions of sculptures were thought of as the end of colonisation. New labels on the same old bottles did not change the wine. The altars were shifted but the collective psyche carried on its worship of the sun it 'knew' now rose in the West. It is little wonder that Chandigarh, Islamabad and Sher Bengal Nagr were planned by the 'best from the West'. Two out of the three were very gifted architects, the third a pathetic exterior decorator, all questionable readers of the culture, and all received with characteristic awe by their ex-servants turned independent clients.

Your Time or Mine?

The civilising alien eventually evacuated the native space mostly reluctantly and sometimes with affected benevolence. The native entered with jubilant excitement, reclaiming his ancestral time. The leaver, however, had locked many chambers on its way out and dug some new labyrinthine dead ends as parting gifts. The enterer found himself standing in a circular hall with distorting mirrors and many doors, some real, but most of them mere mouldings or even cleverly painted illusions. Whether these doors actually opened or not, they all led to chambers of amnesia littered with broken time.

Overcome by this landscape of uncertainty he retracted his path and there stood his old master in the front garden with open arms,

I know you will miss me. But remember it was you who told me to leave. It is no longer politically correct for me to govern you but it is a pleasure to be of ongoing service. We are addicted to one another. Come join the commonwealth of my ex-coolies, come have your picture taken with me. Send me your brightest and I will fill their minds and anoint them with my degrees. They will remind your children of my ancestors. Drink my crystal wine, use your earthen cups, wear your home-spun cottons and raw silk, feel as authentic as you please but remember you need me like the preacher needs the devil. Use my language, insert your words, and then exegesis, sing your poets but quote mine, criticise my philosophies but use them as beacons to locate your own. Take my architecture, play with it if it pleases you, pronounce it your own if you wish, patent your moves, it is quaint to see you act original, authentic, national. Form your own clubs, call them by any archaic names you wish, but always come back to me and my Royal Institute of British Architects, my Commonwealth Association of Architects. One day you might become worthy of my gilded hall of fame. And here are my companions in global adventures of the past. We are the only circus of the present. And we have patents on all the machines that make the future. Together we are the club of moderns. We love to draft humanist manifestos, make socialist declarations and redesign the world. We define, devise, design and then debate. After that we publish our words so that you may know our wisdom. Change is our only constancy. Production is essential to us like swimming to the sharks. Reason and positivist causality reigns supreme among us and self-interest is the only ethic. We uphold freedom, individuality, choice, but we are also certain about what is good for everyone, especially you, you innocent ex-subjects who are not yet ready to make responsible choices. We are the developed ones as must be so obvious to you. You too have to aim to become like us by adopting what we have adopted, discarding what we have discarded. You have to examine your silly old beliefs. Enlightenment that unleashed our future for us and made us worthy of ruling you will for sure one day make you govern your own selves. We are well aware of your tropical vulnerability to lotus-eating, and your general reflective, lazy habits. So, if doing what we did seems very hard work you can always ask us for help. You may even seek associate membership or just come over as guest workers.

National Independent Time

The post-colonial maps were drawn for a complex political and economic agenda. One cannot help noticing a characteristic blindness with which these borders have cut across the cultural continuities that existed across the lands inhabited by Muslim societies. Over the last half-century the new nations have spent much energy play-acting their independence. Much has been consumed in legitimising, making sacred and defending these sovereign enclaves. Their ministries of culture, often sharing a portfolio with tourism, have been busy defining, even fabricating, their unique 'national' identity through paintings, architectural literature and performing arts, all quite analogous to launching national airlines. And in service of this noble cause of inventing national cultures, much historical cut and paste has been patronised or at least tolerated. Many categories in the cultural discourse have been censored and new ones have been inserted. Architecture, the most visible and candid indication of the cultural condition, exhibits many uncomfortable, some absolutely bizarre, compromises between the much envied 'European, Western, Modern' and the politically correct 'National, Eastern, Traditional'. The time that was previously partitioned between the 'native past' rendered irrelevant and the 'European future' declared inevitable, now got cut into numerous national, ethnic and ideological strands. On the game board of competing, sometimes conflicting desires ('renaissance' of Islamic civilisation, political ideology, national identity, technological progress, economic self-reliance, national defence) these strands of time got tangled. While past was the source of legitimacy for this acquired nationhood, the future of this past was confused and suffered from superlative envies of various kinds. Some went for the modernisation and optimisation of the Hajj Terminal and in the process sacrificed much history and heritage of the sacred places. Others, aiming at the return of an Arab and Babylonian glory, sought to build a 'New York on the Tigris'. Still others fabricated dynastic links across the wilderness of time and staged celebrations which would have put the imperial Darbars of Delhi to shame. Architecture of the Muslim societies became a spread-out theme park of distorted memories and fantastic visions with new capital cities, national assemblies, national mosques, university campuses, pan-Islamic institutes and monuments to the wars with neighbours.

Weaving a New Time

The architectural profession, in its varied states of adolescence or reconstruction, was caught in the constant inflow of foreign ideas and images, mostly fashions and trends, through magazines and monographs on the masters, through international consultants and exchange professors. This situation was compounded by packaged graduates coming down the conveyor belts of foreign universities. The construction market, the universities, and the government institutions were all ill-equipped to direct this inflow and allow it to find a fertile basin where an architectural future could blossom. Architecture in these societies started to look like the impromptu bazaar of contraband smuggled goods, curios of alien cultures touted as magic cures for all ills of underdevelopment.

AKAA, 1986, Yaama Mosque, Yaama, Tahoua, Niger

These conditions nourished both cynical pessimism and Utopic optimism among architects. The former led to the abandonment or redefinition of architecture in favour of social causes of employment, housing, health and environment. Architects became public health engineers and advocates of peoples' rights to shelter. Among the Utopians and the like who proposed comprehensive new visions, three were most noticeable. First, the religious revivalist who addressed all philosophical, legal, structural, formal and even aesthetic questions to the Qu'ranic, traditional and the jurisprudential texts. Second, the 'arts and crafts' revivalist of the Islamic kind who proselytised back to earth, gentler, smaller, craft-biased, indigenously rooted communities. And lastly there was the techno-scientific Utopian with attendant geometries, magic materials and novel ways of doing more for less. The apologist for the status quo, superficially using the developmental and evolutionary vocabulary, remained a distracter of these idealists and did everything to marginalise them. The 'foreign', a signifier of high value in the minds of the 'ex-natives', continued to enjoy the veto power over ideas challenging its global hegemonies. And in their own Muslim world the nations went to great lengths to identify themselves as different from their neighbours.

It was in such tangled times of exclusionary national spaces, under the suspicious gaze of the political ideologues and protectors of the purity of the faith, that the Aga Khan Award for Architecture was launched. The first seminar at Aiglemont brought many split personalities of the Muslim psyche face to face. They were eloquent, animated and not always kind to one another. Coming from their secure academies, professorships and practices where they were accepted, even adored by those who surrounded them, they had come to pronounce. They ended up listening to one another, disagreeing with increasing courage, questioning their own assumptions, wondering together. The proceedings were done with honesty not known in the Muslim world. Each one was given a little grey volume as a gift (later editions were done in turquoise); since the change, the present has not been the same.

What started out as a search for the Islamic architecture soon became an archaeology of the Muslim self and its continuity and transformations through time. Muslim past was cut across on numerous planes and discoveries were brought forth, some wishful, mostly as forms and sometimes as values and philosophies. Under the watchful, and not always kind gaze of the professional historians and critics, architects were challenged to reflect upon deeper issues of history, culture, identity, tradition and technology. The notions of boundaries, borders, otherness, difference and their architectural manifestations were brought up. Philosophers were invited to lead the way, keep the image merchants honest and dispel the fog. Over and over again modernity was damned as well as de-fended. Explicit or implicit, links were made between modernity, technology and freedom from dogma. Craft and tradition were put forth as the natural habitat and instrument for Islam. A few years into the Award it finally became possible for the tradition to come out of her romantic chambers of time and meet modernity with expected suspicion and advertised disdain. Modernity, of course, in its self-righteous and patronising manner declared that 'whatever you could do in the past I could do better, faster, cheaper and anywhere'. The debate continues and it is hoped that the dialectic will lead to a higher plateau of mutual awareness. What is important is that the past and present of modernity has been dissected and it is no longer being touted as the exclusive destined future of the Muslims. Post-modernity has often been invoked as an escape through its promise of multiple readings, its assemblage of the discordant, its defence of the historic precedent as an installation, and its promise to blur time. But such are the enchantments of contemporary thought, 'new' criticism and 'new' history. The dams and diversions of alien time – pirates are crumbling from within, and the river is discovering its valley.

Free from the limits of national boundaries, political ideologies, international politics and the revolutionary struggles with the Muslim world itself, the Aga Khan Award has achieved in the past fifteen years what was not possible for national councils, heritage commissions, and alliances like the Arab League, the Organisation of Islamic Conference or even UNESCO to achieve over the past thirty-five years. It has managed to stay free of the dialectics of East and West, of believers and non-believers, of 'us' and the 'others'. It has made sure that it does not lead itself into the strait-jackets of architectural ideologies, manifestos, declarations or charters. It is a banquet set out by an inspired and gracious host. All with the proven love for architecture and genuine commitment to the Muslim future are invited. Imperialists, dormant or otherwise, intolerants of any persuasion, dictators, advertisers, salesmen, and their charlatan companions will find little to their taste here. Wisdom is not on the menu but everyone leaves wiser. History is not served here but one feels the past, present and the future in attendance.

The archaeology of self is turning into an alchemy of ideas that are at peace with Islam. Past is being dusted off as a relevant part of future-making. The fragments of the threadbare, amnesiac past are being knotted around the strings of contemporary time. A new carpet is slowly emerging. The past that was condemned to the silent monuments and the present that was imprisoned in the Euro-American hall of mirrors have met. The progeny has returned to share the banquet with the ancestors. Lutyens and Fletcher have been asked, Ibn Khaldun and Iqbal are scheduled, Ibn Sina is always here, Sinan might pass through but Hassan Fathy has gone on a long journey and cannot come.

FROM ABOVE, L to R: AKAA, National Museum, Doha, Qatar; AKAA, 1986, Dar Lamane, Casablanca, Morocco; AKAA, 1989, Hayy Assafarat, Riyadh, Saudi Arabia; AKAA, 1992, Palace Parks Programme, Istanbul, Turkey

THOUGHTS ON ARCHITECTURE

Turgut Cansever

Architecture in the Islamic world is undergoing a more serious crisis and degeneration than has been experienced by any other culture. It is also obvious that this degeneration cannot be overcome by employing the same means utilised in various other cultures. The Islamic world has experienced a rich variety of cultural and architectural achievements during different periods in its history. Such diversity and richness on the local level, in the context of an overarching whole, is a cultural event unequalled in the history of humanity.

Some of the basic difficulties we face today entail the loss of opportunity to express the Islamic nature of these cultures and works of art, and the question of how best to bring new solutions to the problem of regenerating the great elan and ingenuity of those who have made this diversity possible. The cultural stagnation of production today is not encountered in the Islamic world alone as it is also being experienced in non-Islamic cultures.

From the middle of the nineteenth century, self-assured Western revolutionaries disavowed all historical experience and accumulation, asserting that they possessed everything necessary to reconstruct the world anew, and create a heaven on earth within its frame. Nineteenth-century engineers developed cast-iron and steel construction techniques, claiming they were going to change the future of the world by building a completely new one. Whilst it is true that the world underwent a change never before witnessed in history, this change brought disaster upon the world instead of turning it into Heaven. It has been observed that when socio-economic and technical attempts are made at changing the world, the belief that resolution in one area of existence can result in resolution in every area of existence, is actually the result of attributing divine power as both catalyst and resource.

The whole world has been polluted by the grave miscalculation that the cultural lack of rationality of nineteenth-century eclecticism separated architecture from the material aspects of its technical nature. The architecture of the Islamic world has been alienated from the fundamentals of its own culture and beliefs in addition to the pollution experienced in the West. The devastation caused by the attitude which regards solution devised by others as absolutely valid truths has helped escalate degeneration in these parts of the world.

In the days of emerging totalitarian concepts, when this general degeneration was observed in its major constructs, it was discerned that lack of rationality and detached efforts devoid of 'entirety' would not be able to offer a solution. It became necessary for important steps to be taken in the history of art and the philosophy of art. It was recognised that Hellenistic culture was not the sole cultural achievement of humanity, and by the beginning of the twentieth century it was also accepted that cultures outside the framework of Hellenistic-Christian cultures deserved to be surveyed and measured within their own evaluation systems.

The fact that the quality of art could not be determined with the form of description of archeology was appreciated apart from the contributions of the psychological, aesthetic school. Heinrich Wolfflin, by comparing the Renaissance and Baroque arts and starting with the considerations which provided the stylistic attributes, presented the art which he thought had universal validity. He also pointed out that the form categories determining Renaissance and Baroque arts belong to two different systems of belief. He then asserted that it was imperative to enter into the relation between the culture, its system of belief and art forms, to remain within the sphere of art.

In the dynamic thinking environment of the beginning of this century, the German historian of art Alois Riegl, determined the relationship between the changes taking place in the Roman culture and art form. Ludwig Coellen posited the second important explanation to the genetics of aesthetics. He approached it from three perspectives: the creation of the form characteristics of the work of art; the factors which bring about its style; and the genetics of how art and style originated in Western Europe.

Ernst Diez's study, 'A Stylistic Analysis of Islamic Art, Simultaneity in Islamic Art' (1938), followed the work of Riegel and Coellen in the area of genetics of aesthetics. While his study offered new horizons for understanding the genetics of aesthetics, it also contained the outlook of linear evolvement contradictory to reality. The latter had been developed by the Archeological Institute of Vienna (of which Diez was a member), and was a dominant idea in Western Europe. It asserted that works of art could only be evaluated together with the basic beliefs and judgements of the culture in which they had evolved.

AKAA, 1992, Demir Holiday Village, Mugla, Turkey

AKAA, 1989, Rehabilitation of Asilah, Asilah, Morocco

Such an attitude is also present in describing the native cultures of Africa and America as primitive and backward, a similar approach displayed in a series of misconceptions of value expressed by Diez, which has led to other misjudgments connected with this process. The Wolfflin categories take a similar view, limiting themselves to analysing the form features of the shape of the works of art and leaving out the relation between the work of art and human beings, and the problems connected with the creative period of the work of art. It is also not sufficient to find an explanation for the problems of art in all the epochs with figuration categories, based on the form qualities such as 'definiteness' and 'indefiniteness' – attributes of both the Renaissance and Baroque cultures.

However, the assertion was that replacement of the expression of art with those belonging to the sphere of culture would make it possible to move outside the sphere of the essential problem of art, thus moving away from the sphere of the essential problem. This assertion has proven to be a grave misapprehension. The appropriateness of the criticism directed towards psychological aesthetics is due to the fact that psychological aesthetics regard this aspect of the work of art as the only factor constituting the style of the work of art. It is also a result of not taking into consideration the entirety of the various problems related to different existence levels. In the atmosphere of these misapprehensions and the voids which have lasted throughout the century, it is obvious that the contributions of the genetics of aesthetics and existentialist philosophy have been considerable and of special importance.

Throughout its history, Western philosophy has been confronted with unsolvable problems because of the concept of existence as consisting of two strata, the material and the spiritual. In actual fact, the new ontology has defined existence as material, biological, spiritual and moral. In addition to the explanations concerning the order of the relations between these strata of existence, it is obvious that the concept of wholeness forms the most important basis for genetics of aesthetics. It contributes greatly to the history of art and, even more importantly, to the solutions that can be brought to the problems of art and especially to the problems encountered in the project phase of architecture.

In particular, there is the simultaneous contemplation of Diez regarding 'place' and 'time' throughout history: the structure of the whole, the relationship between the part and the whole, the organic and the cumulative wholeness, the static and the moving, the simple and polar compositions formed through the direct and the indirect polar reflections of the transcendental structures on the objective universe. His explanation of the ornamental subject, while introducing invaluable principles for the comprehension of the history of art anew, based on these foundations, considerably facilitates the comprehension of Islamic art and architecture.

Apart from this event, there are the studies of Amanda Coomaraswamy and Titus Burckhardt on the problems connected with the relation of man as spectator or as a living being when faced with works of art, and especially when facing architecture. Their work, emphasising the religious and cultural attributes gained by the work of art according to the faith of the artist creating it, has revealed new dimensions of this problem. Since the beginning of this century, the relationship between the quality of the work of art, and what it is made of, has remained on the agenda. Specifically in architecture, construction materials, technology and the reality concerning the importance of the factors belonging to the material sphere of existence, while becoming almost a sole determination and a divinity which would solve everything, the invalidity of the claims to absolute perfection, was brought to the agenda in the 1960s. The myriad of coincidences that occurred during the emergence of the work of art and architecture replaced the central reason and authority. It also had an effect on the quality of the work of art, on the contributions of human beings at every level, and on what the role of the human beings who are elements of the emergence, and consequently, what their rights are going to be. All these were also on the agenda.

The criticism brought to the raising of the collective work of Walter Gropius and the architects in his circle, to the status of a 'prima donna' at the beginning of the century, has remained ineffective throughout the century.

On the one hand, the image of the architects of 'prima donna' architecture dominates – which emerged as a result of the approach of central decision and preferences which reigned. On the other hand, after the Second World War, as a result of the socialism which was the outcome of Anglo-Saxon empiricism and pragmatism, the problems of linguistics in connection with those of the symbols appeared on the current agenda. Research on the mechanisms of production of man in reaching the level of being a work of art, and the genetics of the work of art, has been removed from the agenda completely in the years following the Second World War. After the War, while the question of what the new structure of Islamic art and architecture should be – with the zeal obtained when their political independence on the scene of the world politics was placed on the agenda – the habit in Islamic countries of following the stride of one or the other developments mentioned above continued.

However, there were attempts to elucidate the questions relating to the origin of the Abstract Geometrical Ornamentation, which is a manifestation of Islamic art unequalled in the history of humanity, using Islamic cosmology as the starting point. This approach did not include the form qualities inborn in a being, although it had been possible to be aware of them, manifesting the divine command of the Prophet, who said in connection with these natural qualities, 'look at everything, look at the Sun, the Moon, the stars, the earth, the water, and the grass'. Apart from the reality that these holy qualities imparted to Islamic art, departing from this reality could only elucidate a limited aspect of Islamic art. Neither did it include the concept of place-being, which was brought to the agenda through the genetics of aesthetics and subjects such as organic or cumulative wholeness, movement and statism, simple and polar compositions, ornamentalism, and so on. Besides these, the material, technical, bio-social forms and the qualities of the shapes that have a decision-forming significance specifically for architecture, and which Paul Klee defined in gross outline as silence, peace, harmony, contradiction, etc, correspond to psychic states, manifestations and faiths regarding the concepts of the creation of man, the universe and existence, and how the choices determined by cosmic sensation came to be and how this determined the style of art.

The topic of how the universe created by God and the will of God which is manifest in every sphere of existence, could be reached and conformed to; how the rule of Islam that the command of God is to be obeyed unconditionally is to be actualised; and how this could be achieved by making whole the information about the formation of exigence, and the information about the genetics of art – all this could be cleansed of its misconceptions and not brought to the agenda.

The truth of the oneness of God and, consequently, the unity of existence needs to be emphasised. It needs to be said that the solutions offered which are based on limited subjects and spheres turn into idols, each and every one. It is observed in the West as well as the Islamic world (which has been inclined to follow the stride of the Western example, especially during the last 150 years) that these solutions are the result of the gravest misjudgement, which most definitely needs to be overcome.

During periods of twenty to thirty years, the pulling down of the idols of these false solutions that are almost worshipped by everyone, and the new ones being constructed to replace them, has been praised. This procedure has being interpreted as dynamic and creative, and the resulting state of irrationalty has dragged the world down into a swamp of pollution The way to overcome these short-term analyses and solutions can be found in examining history in its entirety, thereby searching for solutions which have a genuinely lasting effect.

Solutions which are long-lasting can only be founded upon a mutual basis of consistent totalitarian information and faith. It is obvious that a comparative history of art and architecture could offer great contributions.

In order for lasting resolutions to continue between the contrasting characters of the cultures of the wholly colourless and uneasy, and the human cultures of the Middle Ages and the Baroque which devoted a lot of time to dramatic and tragic subjects, solutions have to be found which take into account the realities of coming into being.

The realisation of these two poles together constitute the source, the unequalled phenomena in the history of mankind. It speaks of variety, regional differentiation, and the entirety of the Islamic culture.

Instead of a self-centred, static, dull entirety, a dynamic, open, cumulative entirety is motivated to meet the needs of the aspect of the existence, located forever in a state of becoming. Produced with the tectonics that are the foundation stones of entirety, taking place in the infinitive space as responsible beings, there would be an imperative and a reflection of the concept of 'Complete Man' which will illuminate mankind again.

It is absolutely necessary that the effects directed at offsetting the destructive conflict caused by the turmoil of the individualistic approach to the twentieth century, and the standards formed based on narrow points of view, should proceed in the direction suggested by this analysis.

FURTHER READING

1   Ludwig Coellen, *Der Still*, Der Bilqenden Kunt Arkaden Verlag Traisa, Darmstad, 1921.
2   Heinrich Wolfflin, *Principles of Art History*, Dover Productions Inc, New York .
3   Worriger, *L'Art Gothique*, Gallimard, Paris, 1946.
4   Enst Diez, *A Stylistic Analysis of Islamic Art; Ornamentalism in Islamic Art; Simultaneity in Islamic Art*, Ars Islamic, Michigan, 1938.
5   Amanda K Coomaraswamy, *Christian and Oriental Philosophy*, Dover Publications Inc, New York.
6   Mazar Sevket Ibsiroglu, *Gotik San'at*, Guzel San'atlar Mecmuasi, Istanbul, 1942.
7   Titus Burckhardt, *Principes et methodes de l'art sacre*, Devry-Livres, Paris, 1976.
8   Fusus Ul-Hikemr, *Muhiddin-i Arabi*, Milli Egitim Basimevi, Istanbul, 1952.

CONSERVATION IN THE ISLAMIC WORLD

Ronald Lewcock

The clash between the aims of cultural conservation and the desire for modernisation has become a serious issue in light of the steadily diminishing residues of heritage, particularly in urban areas, leading to an increasing rejection of traditional values by many classes of society. The effects of these clashes are now at their most severe in the cities of Africa and Asia, where until recently the pace of modernisation was slow and societies were conservative. The last decade has seen a marked change in that situation, a change I have been particularly concerned with as an architect active in architectural and urban conservation and rehabilitation in those continents.

The new admiration for Western technology and culture has resulted in a sense of inferiority in many Islamic countries, sowing seeds of doubt about the value of their own achievements. A reaction against traditional society and traditional patterns of living has meant that it is difficult to persuade many people that their own culture is worth preserving. The effect of this new feeling is especially profound in architecture. Destruction is produced not only through demolition but, as often as not, through tasteless remodelling and – even if the buildings are preserved – through a complete change in their setting. Multi-storey buildings now cluster around old mosques, which were once the most important and highest buildings in the landscape, their minarets lost amongst the skyscrapers.

Inhabitants of traditional Islamic countries cannot easily be convinced that the value of a building in its old form should over-ride its remodelling in the techniques of Western technology. This is partly because a genuine feeling of humility and modesty makes them under-rate their own traditional buildings. The more recently a building was built, the more serious this problem is likely to be. To persuade someone that buildings three or four hundred years old should be preserved is not difficult as they are rare in any case. The problem is to persuade governments and ordinary people that the value of a building is not measured by its age in a traditional society where building traditions and patterns of use have been maintained for centuries without change. A building one-generation old can be important, not only as a representative of a traditional style, but because it suits the needs of, and therefore facilitates, the sustaining in an active state of the handicrafts and ways of life of the society.

Contemporary city administrators and regional and urban planners are loathe to become involved in cultural conservation or the adaptive reuse of old buildings, neighbourhoods or city centres: the administrators, because the patterns of land ownership, rehousing, fixed rents and political ramifications among the people are often daunting; and the planners, because almost all their training is in the provision of new suburbs or new towns on virgin sites – they have practically no conceptual training in ways of improving existing urban fabrics of old types. Indeed the gulf between the Utopian ideologies of the new planners and the practical common sense fabrics that have evolved over centuries is extreme. Most planners simply do not know how to make the adjustment; they are unable to perceive, or unwilling to admit, the very real values inherent in traditional patterns.

On a practical level, both the politicians and the planners would generally prefer to clear an area in order to begin anew without all the attendant problems, complexities and unfamiliarities that urban and building conservation involves.

However, the total clearing of an area itself entails political repercussions. Sometimes, to avoid these the politicians and the planners are content with road widening or, even worse, with driving wide roads through traditional areas. Where individual buildings are thought to be of particular value they may be moved out of the way in their entirety (as was the case with the beautiful fourteenth-century mosque opposite Bab Zuwayla in Cairo). More often than not, however, the building is truncated so that a range of its rooms simply disappears completely, and the facade is rebuilt near the centre of its original plan. Where repairs are done to the public buildings or houses affected by road widening, the facades are moved back in this way – or worse, inferior makeshift facades replace the originals.

The effect of wide roads on the traditional fabric is generally catastrophic. The intimacy of the spaces in old cities was a reflection of the ease of interaction among its people, something which is unthinkable, let alone practicable, across wide roads filled with fast-moving traffic or through areas of parked cars. Furthermore, the relatively

PREVIOUS PAGE: AKAA, 1986, Restoration of al-Aqsa Mosque, Jerusalem; FROM ABOVE: Interior of the dome of the al-Aqsa Mosque, Jerusalem; detail showing the 'before and after' effects of restoration work in the al-Aqsa Mosque

narrow streets of traditional cities in hot climates ensured that they were in shade for a large part of each day, and therefore neither the people nor the buildings were exposed to the sun. Narrow sidestreets provided secluded, semi-private access spaces to neighbourhoods, which facilitated a sense of community and the enjoyment of life. With the intrusion of the motorcar, these lanes have become blocked, impassable and alien. Widening them, or knocking down buildings to provide parking spaces, does nothing to restore the communal seclusion and cohesion. In such developments, monuments become isolated instead of part of the continuous urban fabric.

Indeed, one of the characteristics of modernisation is a policy of deliberately isolating monuments that were never meant to be seen in isolation. The sea of parked cars around them is often the *coup de grace* to their original character.

There are also technical problems introduced by modernisation. Apart from pollution from the noxious gases produced by industry and vehicle exhausts, which accelerates the decay of building surfaces at an extraordinarily rapid rate, there are other alarming effects introduced by the modernisation of the urban environment.

One of the most visible of the technical problems, as well as one of the most serious, is the extent to which dampness is rising to unprecedented levels in the buildings. The reason for this can be stated very simply in each rapidly growing city: as the population density has gone up, water has been made available to more people in much greater quantities than ever before; but the infrastructure for draining that water out of the various areas of the city has usually not been supplied, or, if it has, has not been adequate in size or standard.

Consequently, the water draining into the ground creates a new 'perched' water table on top of the fine layer of clays accumulated from centuries of human habitation. This new water table gradually rises up to the point at which it causes damage to the buildings. In many cases the water is continually coming out at ground level to create pools in the streets. Water rising in the walls causes tremendous damage; add the fact that it is water polluted with acids from human and animal excrement and the problems increase. This is clearly, then, a major problem that must be solved in conserving buildings or rehabilitating an old area, because the cost of rectifying it represents a major part of the total cost of any conservation or rehabilitation programme.

Another problem confronting efforts at conservation is traffic circulation. Not only does vibration destroy the individual buildings, but the increased number of motorised vehicles has tyrannised pedestrians and the narrow market streets have become impassable. Cars and trucks are parked everywhere, blocking the passages. Yet means have to be found of allowing cars and delivery vehicles into the old cities. One method being tried out is to allow traffic to a very limited number of streets in the old city and to limit the access of vehicles in the rest of the streets in the same area to restricted times at night and in the morning. Whether these policies are enforceable in many of the Islamic countries is another matter.

On a more hopeful note, this may be the place to interrupt this catalogue of disasters with the observation that all of the issues dealt with so far are also experienced and solved in non-Islamic countries. In the effort to Westernise, the Islamic world tends to overlook the fact that many Western countries are actively engaged in protecting their past and are making huge efforts to preserve their traditional environments. Germany, Holland, Italy, France, Poland, Czech and Slovak countries, to name but a few, have confronted and largely solved many of their seemingly intractable problems.

To return to the issues confronting conservation, deterioration from lack of maintenance is yet another major concern. Buildings constructed in the traditional ways in the Islamic world were meant to be maintained. It was an accepted part of life that, after the rains, repainting and replastering would be needed to repair any water damage, for if this was not done every year, deterioration would be extraordinarily rapid. Now annual maintenance is no longer an accepted part of life, and the consequences are severe. First the roofs decay, then the corners crack and fall away because the walls have been damaged by the rains. In no time at all fairly respectable multi-storey buildings become ruined single-storey structures. They are left as single-storey buildings and not allowed to totally collapse, simply because shopkeepers and craftspersons occupy the ground floor, and their rent in most traditional societies represents the bulk of the profit on a building investment. It is therefore in everyone's interest, including the owners', to maintain the ground floors. They waterproof the floors of what were once the first storeys (ie, the ceilings of the ground floor), which have consequently become the roofs of the buildings.

Nor is this process limited to unprofitable rental buildings, where decaying structures can be attributed to the grasping mentality of landlords who allow their buildings to decay because the rents are too low. It is happening to some of the major monuments of Islam. In Cairo, probably thirty percent of the waqf properties in the old city are shrinking storey by storey; some have already reached the ground-floor level, with ghostly walls rising up three or four floors. In one waqf property in Cairo, in the canvas-makers' *suq* near the Bab Zuwayla, the upper levels of the *suq* – once beautifully designed and comfortable waqf houses – have all been allowed to decay. Yet this *suq* has always been regarded by everybody concerned with conservation in Cairo as one of the major monuments. We must come to terms with the principle of annual maintenance if we are going to talk about preserving and upgrading Islamic cities.

Natural disasters also pose more than just the obvious conservation problems. We tend to think only of immediate problems and ignore potential ones. In many areas of the Middle East, for example, flooding is frequent but not usually very serious as it can be controlled with diversion dams. Once every thirty, fifty or one hundred years, however, a major flood occurs. Everybody knows there will be one because the city has been washed away regularly once or twice a century for a thousand years. Nobody does anything about it, however, and one of the first priorities of any conservation scheme should be to take steps to anticipate the problem. Similarly, although there may not have been a major earthquake for decades or centuries, history tells us that they are possible throughout most of the Islamic world. Conservation efforts need to anticipate this possibility as well.

Land tenure in Muslim societies, as we know, is very different from that in the West. One of the ways it differs is that the people used to be responsible for the maintenance of the street in front of their houses. Street cleaning was a traditional task of the inhabitants of the abutting houses. These customs have rapidly fallen away in the last twenty years – in some places as recently as during the last six or seven years. In many old cities the inhabitants say, 'We're now living in modern states, we have powerful central governments, why should we continue to perform such tasks?' And so the litter accumulates, and the best intentioned efforts of municipal governments to provide cleaning and collecting facilities have yet to succeed.

Another aspect of land tenure – joint ownership due to inheritance – poses still other problems. Even buildings regarded as national monuments can be privately owned, and private ownership can involve so many members of a family that the protection and maintenance of the monument can be prevented through lack of agreement or for want of a single person to take responsibility.

In promoting conservation as one of the aspects of the Aga Khan Award, the organisers have attempted to focus attention upon the need to address such problems. Awards are given to projects which have developed conservation strategies which promise to be successful, and might therefore be studies as models for other projects. Some of these are discussed below.

The Shah Rukn-i-'Alam tomb in Multan, Pakistan, dominates the city from a site high on the former citadel. Its dilapidated state, before conservation was undertaken, had a depressing effect on an ancient but vital city of craftsmen and artists. The tomb was conserved by architect Walli Ullah Khan in an exemplary fashion, using traditional techniques almost exclusively. A major effort was made to locate craftsmen who understood the ancient techniques of tile making and even more important, to locate sources of the mineral deposits for the unique coloured glazes of the craftsmen who originally made tiles for the tomb, six hundred years earlier; one such crafts-

OPPOSITE: AKAA, 1983, The Azem Palace, Damascus, Syria; ABOVE: AKAA, 1989, Rehabilitation of Asilah, Asilah, Morocco

man was found, and using his knowledge it proved possible to revive a craft which seemed completely lost. The unique heritage of the tomb decoration was restored in all its original glory. This work was preceded by the most painstaking reconstruction and strengthening of the original structure and repair of its brickwork. Although the tomb has been so thoroughly restored that some of its patina of age has been lost, the great achievement of the conservation project was twofold: a major medieval craft industry in Multan has been revived and continues to flourish, and the tomb today is revealed for the first time in centuries as one of the great achievements of Islamic architecture on the Indian subcontinent.

The Azem Palace in Damascus occupies a historic site in the ancient *suq* area close to the great Omayyad Mosque of al-Walid. As the largest accessible private dwelling in the historic centre, a focus for the revival of arts and crafts as well as a museum of traditional culture, its deplorable condition had become a symbol of decline in the old city. It was the dedication of the curator of the museum in the palace, Shafiq al-Imam, which led to its successful conservation. He supervised each stage of the work and undertook the location and training of the craftsmen employed on it. The result is the return to its full beauty of one of the most magnificent examples of the legendary Damascus Islamic palaces.

The third award was to a scheme that was actually intended by its sponsors, the German Archaeological Institute in Cairo, to have a direct impact on urban rehabilitation in the old city. By selecting five historic buildings for conservation in one traditional quarter, they hoped to provide the people of the neighbourhood exemplars and encouragement to undertake the renovation of their own houses. It was thought that such a seed planted in the old city might grow and spread to other areas. Here, the conservation work was initially undertaken by an architectural historian, Michael Meinecke, who achieved remarkable success with the first building to be renovated, the Madrasa al-Anuki. Subsequently, a young architect, Philip Speiser, joined Dr Meinecke on the work and completed the projects. The work of this team was characterised by the great care taken to locate and use the last of the master craftsmen surviving in Cairo, and by the willingness of the architects to learn traditional techniques and implement them wherever possible. It is notable that the money received from the Award was itself used to undertake another major conservation project adjoining the earlier work, the renovation of the Madrasa of Mohammed Nasr.

The first project for the conservation of an entire old city centre to receive an Aga Khan Award was that of Mostar in Yugoslavia in 1986. Here, one man, Dzihad Pasic, who had formerly been a regional conservation officer, took the initiative by forming an organisation, Stari-Grad, which persuaded the municipality of Mostar to waive taxes and concede control of services in a small area on either side of the famous single-span bridge crossing the Neretva River. While the buildings and streets were being brought back to the appearance they had a century earlier, the bridge itself was thoroughly studied and conserved. The demonstrable success of this first phase made it relatively easy for Pasic to persuade the authorities to grant him the same opportunities in a further thirty buildings surrounding the first zone. The enthusiasm engendered by this phase in visitors and townspeople alike enabled him to further extend his operations until, at the outbreak of the Yugoslavian Civil War, the entire area of the seventeenth-century town was part of the conservation scheme. By conserving, renovating and in a few cases, reconstructing, the old commercial and residential buildings of the town, Stari-Grad was able to finance conservation work on streets, services and public monuments. This demonstration of the self-sustaining ability of urban conservation was unfortunately brought to an end by the conflict in his country, with Mostar suffering more damage than many other centres. It is to be hoped that the strong condition to which the buildings had been returned will have reduced the damage they might otherwise have received, and that the example of Stari-Grad's work will inspire the eventual restoration of Mostar and many other towns like it in that country.

Also given an Aga Khan Award in 1986 was the conservation of the most hallowed shrines in the Islamic world, the al-Aqsa Mosque adjoining the Dome of the Rock in Jerusalem. The Award initiation stressed the restoration work on the dome of the mosque, which had deteriorated so far that water leakage had effectively obliterated the valuable painted decoration on the inner surface. All this was saved, the roof reconstructed, the paintings returned to their former glory, and the work extended to encompass the whole of the rest of the mosque and the structures of the gates and fountains of the Haram beyond. Encouraged by the Award, conservation of the great building of the Dome of the Rock itself is now being studied and considered.

The reconstruction and conservation of the Great Omari Mosque in the Lebanese city of Sidon received an Award in 1989, as did a second urban rehabilitation scheme, that of Asilah in Morocco. Interest in this old city had been generated by making it the focus of an annual Arts Festival, which, though small at first, became the biggest cultural event in Morocco and one of the most important in the Arab world. Impetus and the means to undertake the rehabilitation followed naturally.

In 1992 an Award was given to the strategy adopted in Kairouan in Tunisia of stimulating pride in an historic area and catalysing its rehabilitation through the conservation of key monuments. Funds for the conservation were obtained solely from entrance fees to the monuments. Many of the twelve conserved buildings were modified so that they could house new functions, such as a school for deaf children, social services and so on, which would keep them active in the life of the community and ensure that their rehabilitation would have maximum repercussions. The expertise and experiences gained were then made available for the renovation of private dwellings. The physical welfare, training and employment of the inhabitants were improved, as well as the visual attraction of the city to residents and visitors.

In Istanbul an initiative of the Towring Organisation in repairing hotels, villas and small quarters of the old city and its neighbouring villages received recognition in 1986, and in 1992 the programme of the National Palaces Trust in repairing and opening to the public the eight palaces and thirty gardens of the Ottoman Sultans received an Award. Each was accorded new functions so that it took a place in the social life of the surrounding area and city.

The view that conservation is inevitably expensive has been revised recently in the light of a number of significant developments. Since the jolt given to the building industries of Western countries following the oil crisis of 1973, it has been found that renovation of old buildings is now generally cheaper than the construction of new ones – resulting in a major turn around in attitudes to rehabilitation and conservation. To this have been added new studies by the World Bank and other agencies of the economic benefits that might accrue to poor countries by consolidating their building stock, and from the introduction of innovative policies of incentive to encourage regeneration in old cities as well as new constructions.

To conclude, we should consider responses to those sceptics who question the value of conservation in resource-poor developing societies. In addition to preserving some of the world's important cultural heritage, conservation carries four benefits with it: identity, self-respect, pride and utility.

A sense of identity needs to be generated afresh to counteract the alienating effects produced in many a people by the too-rapid changes of modern life. Paying attention to continuity in the environment can help to do that. Self-respect is being destroyed as people see their values and lifestyle being denigrated in favour of imported ideas; preserving contexts of national or regional lifestyles may help to build it again. Only one step beyond this is the positive cultivation of pride in the achievement of one's forebears and in the unique heritage that they have passed on to their descendants.

Social anthropologists reason that culture is a complex and fundamental part of the human spirit, much of it appreciated and relied upon subconsciously. It may be tampered with only at the peril of the whole society. And many believe that the man-made environment is one of the major artefacts among the cultural achievements of society. Hence its conservation is of great significance.

I have put utility last. The benefits of studies of function come firstly from practical observations of the lessons of the past: how harsh climates were dealt with; how people built when there was little choice but to rely on local materials and technologies; and how social tensions were accommodated and communal cohesiveness cultivated through the forms generated in the environment. Practical utilitarian benefits may also be achieved by observing that valuable commercial processes – the production of crafts and the provision in a traditional *suq* of a vast diversity of goods – are facilitated by special building conformations evolved over centuries. Utilitarian benefits might also include some investment return through tourism – although this is a mixed benefit which needs to be carefully handled.

The clash between cultural conservation and modernisation should be a thing of the past. Today conservation is seen as being as one with development, an integral and inevitable partnership. Only in this way will the human and material resources of a country be fully utilised.

EXPRESSING AN ISLAMIC IDENTITY
MOSQUES BUILT IN WESTERN SOCIETIES

Hasan-Uddin Khan

The modern encounter of Muslims and the West started over a century ago but only began to take form after many of the countries with majority Muslim populations achieved independence in the late 1940s and the 1950s – the phase of nationalism. A second phase of the encounter – internationalism – took place in the 1970s with ideas of progress and economic and cultural independence taking on a new guise. A recent third phase – Islamisation – may be discerned since the late 1980s where Islam has increasingly become a defining force in evolving political agendas, not only in the Middle East but from North and West Africa to the Central Asian republics of the former Soviet Union, from India to Western China and in South-East Asia. This phase varies from the Islamic experience of the 1970s and early 1980s (Iran in 1979, Lebanon after 1982 or Egypt in the late 1970s, etc) in that, in general, change is being advocated from within existing political systems and is more prevalent amongst the mainstream Sunni who account for at least eighty-five percent of the world's one billion Muslims. This assertion of identity within what one can call an Islamist tradition, tests not only the expressions of Islamic nation-states but also that of individual and collective aspirations.[1]

The expression of identity can be perceived in many ways – perhaps one that is clearest and most apparent is its manifestation in architecture. Identity is tested when contexts and boundaries of definition change; for instance, when one becomes a 'foreigner'. The notion of building boundaries as a means of self-definition is common in anthropology and sociology, and in terms of identifying oneself in relationship to the 'other'.[2] What a foreigner builds in his or her adopted land is an externalising of identity, which is what I shall explore here through the public aspect of the religious and social life of Muslims in non-Muslim societies – the mosques.

From the onset of mercantile development after 1815, the cities to which immigrants came were less and less places of settled native populations. Urban migration and its attendant economics was one of the forces that fostered nationalism; an image of some place fixed for those who were experiencing displacement. This movement of people set against an enduring land, of economic redeployment and migration of labour which began in the mid-nineteenth century, is likely to continue in our ever-globalising world. The motives for cultural idealisation may be even stronger for us than it was for people who lived through the first great age of industrial capitalism in the nineteenth century. The era of the 'universal citizen' celebrated by Kant was an era which could not conceive of mass migration and cultural instability of the extent we see in the twentieth century.[3]

In today's world in which material culture and intellectual paradigms are shifting away from manifestations of the nation state and industrialisation, perhaps a different lens is needed with which to view the international settlements of people and what they represent, both from an individual and community perspective.[4] The 'foreigner', foreign to the other inhabitant of the shared space, is in a curious position: he or she cannot become a universal citizen, cannot throw off the mantle of nationalism and can only cope with the heavy baggage of culture – but subjects it to certain kinds of displacement to lighten its burdensome weight. The need to be a participant in the 'project of modernity' and yet remember one's own traditions lies at the root of expressing an Islamic identity through buildings. It is an act of displacement which often produces curious results when Asians and Africans live in Western societies. This effort to displace the imagery of tradition and culture is similar to the work of twentieth-century artists whose energies have been marshalled not so much to represent objects but to displace them.

The notion of the altered context, both operational and physical, also plays an important role in this expression of change. Boundaries are being dissolved both intellectually and in reality, but are being replaced with others, making a 'difference' in the expressions of identity and self here to stay in the foreseeable future.[5]

One can look at the phenomenon of displacement, of transformation and of change expressed through building from that of a regionalist's perspective. By regional, I am referring here to building types that have existed in a society over a period of time, long enough to have established a tradition in terms of image, style, function, technology and construction. However, due to mass communications and the international transmission of ideas, it now appears impossible not to be influenced by international developments and to base buildings strictly

on a local or regional tradition. Hence, the notion of an 'authentic' expression of culture in today's world is hard to define; and this becomes even more difficult when different cultures come into contact with each other. In fact, can we understand what is authentic in another culture from the viewpoint of our own? Do we really understand what is authentic about our buildings? I am reminded of a description by William Carlos Williams in *America and Alfred Stieglitz*, where he writes: 'They saw birds with rusty breasts and called them robins. Thus from the start, an America of which they could have no inkling drove the first settlers upon their past. They retreated for warmth and reassurance to something previously familiar but at a cost. For what they saw were not robins'.[6] The example is slight but interesting enough to illustrate how outsider viewpoints can alter meanings. It has its parallel in architecture: do we know how to read the architecture of a place that is not our own?

Architecture is interpretation and mediates realities. Buildings, by their very state of being, communicate directly to people. Creating an environment that 'feels right' raises the question of simulation. The questions of how we judge are these: how do we judge a satisfying mendacity? How do we, in an increasingly global culture in which regions are not easily definable, project the authenticity of locality? What relationship does the architectural expression in a new situation have with the object 'back home', born within a definable architectural tradition? To speak of inheriting and extending a tradition, sometimes into different realms, does not mean copying what has gone before but of absorbing the principles behind earlier solutions and transforming them into new vocabularies suitable to changed attitudes. It gives rise to ideas of transfer and transformation that begin to address issues of understanding and operation in cultures other than our own. For regional architecture, or indeed new architecture, to express cultural roots, what may be called the 'deep structures' have not only to be transferred, but also transformed, if they are to take root in new situations.

Manifestations of a self-conscious identity and the role as self-conscious guardians of Islam relates individual experience to community. Muslims entering a community in the West express their collective identity most clearly through the mosques that they commission. In general, these 'symbolic' mosques are found in cities and are built by Muslims of different origins and backgrounds, serving as indicators of how a particular religious group sees itself within a new or different cultural setting. These may be distinguished from mosques built by communities for their own everyday use, such as the African-American storefront mosques in Philadelphia or New York, or local buildings such as the Islamic Centre in Plainfield, Indiana, or Sherefudin's White Mosque in Visoko, Bosnia. It can be argued that the older immigrant populations, such as those in Britain (like the Black Muslims of the United

States) are now an integral part of English settlements and that their expressions of identity cannot be seen as expressions of 'the other' within their adopted homeland. However, I believe that the process of assimilation is nowhere near complete and that the different Muslim populations, such as the Pakistanis living in England, still, by and large, view themselves as apart and distinct from 'the British'.[7] Hence, the characterisation of the expression of 'difference' and a separate reality still holds even in such long-standing situations.

Projects for mosques expressing Muslim presence in non-Islamic countries started to take shape in the 1950s, although there are earlier examples. However, the colonial connections between countries like Britain and India, France and Algeria, or Italy and Libya remained. Early mosques, like England's first purpose-built mosque in Woking, Surrey, founded in 1889 by Shah Jehan Begum, the wife of the then Nawab of Bhopal, was a version of the Indian Mughal mosques of Lahore and Delhi. Similarly, the Paris Mosque built in the late 1920s was modelled on North African architecture. By the 1960s the burgeoning immigrant Muslim communities in Europe and North America began to express their identity and existence through building new mosques. Projects that had been initiated in the 1950s, like the Islamic Centre in Hamburg, built between 1960 and 1973, and funded jointly by the Iranian community in Germany and religious institutions in Iran, were finally seeing the light of day.

Like their counterparts in Islamic countries – the state and local authority sponsored mosques – mosques built in foreign cultural settings are characterised by four tendencies. Firstly, they accommodate multiple social and cultural activities as well as religious activities, and house facilities such as libraries and nurseries. Secondly, their design is tempered by the local context, modified by local laws and regulations, and sometimes by local community pressures. Thirdly, the design refers back to historical or regional Islamic traditions and the physical form is usually influenced by one dominant style from a country or region, depending on who is financing, designing or leading the project. Lastly, the interiors of the prayer halls tend to be exuberant and often eclectic collections of styles and ornament that proclaim the space as being particularly Islamic. The following examples are presented as outline case studies, emblematic of the periods and images that Muslims wish to project to society at large.[8]

In the United States, the 1957 Islamic Center in Washington DC was established by a group of Muslim ambassadors stationed in the capital some fourteen years after its inception. The project is particularly remarkable for the perseverance of the initiators and for its breadth of vision. In addition to religious and prayer-related facilities, the scope of the initial project included a wide range of services such as a museum; an institute of higher learning for history, art, *sharia*, Arabic and religious studies for

children; an academic magazine and various publications dealing with Islamic issues, lectures and library facilities. Many of the clients' objectives were never fulfilled due to lack of funds, personnel, space and some divisions within the Muslim community itself. It is probably the first such centre in the United States (although the first mosque designed as such in North America seems to have been in Ontario, Canada at the turn of the century). It is interesting to note that the inception of the idea was contemporaneous with that of the London Central Mosque, and that the two undertakings influenced each other in community action, though not in design.

The site of the Washington mosque is in the prominent heart of the embassy quarter of Massachusetts Avenue. During the long years it took to realise the building, many Muslim countries, persuaded by their diplomats, substantially funded the works which were also supported by donations by individuals and communities both in North America and abroad.[9] The Egyptian ambassador persuaded the Egyptian Ministry of Waqf to design the centre. In Cairo, the Ministry assigned an Italian architect, Mario Rossi, residing and employed by the Ministry of Works, to design the Centre. Rossi was an influential architect who had designed several mosques in Egypt. His design shows an adherence to tradition using the Ottoman centralised dome type, stylistically reflecting Cairene models.

Fronting onto the avenue, the building is reached by a flight of steps that lead to a main colonnaded portico entrance, decorated with a tall band of calligraphy. The building is two storeys high with pointed arch windows on the second floor, covered by a sloping green-tiled roof reminiscent of Andalusian architecture. The whole structure is crowned by crenallations and by a fifty metre (160 foot) high Mamluk-inspired minaret. As a result of the zoning requirements in Washington, the building had to be modified, especially in its alignment with the street – causing the entrance facade and the prayer hall's Mecca orientation to create an angled courtyard transitioned space. The actual prayer hall for eight hundred worshippers is almost square in plan and covered by a dome. The lower part of the external walls are ornately decorated with a band of Turkish tiles based on Iznik designs (donated by the Turkish government), as is the *mihrab* which is treated as an arched niche. Next to it, the *minbar* (donated by the Egyptian government) consists of thousands of pieces of hand-carved wood, inlaid with bone and ivory. The eighteen metre (sixty foot) high dome is supported on an octagonal drum with arched windows, on a square base which in turn is on stone columns. Egyptian craftsmen executed the plaster work and the calligraphy which features Qur'anic verses and the names of Allah, the Prophet and the four Caliphs in Kufic script. At the time of the Center's construction, the question of whether to admit women to prayer remained unresolved, but today a small curtained space is provided for them.

Another mosque that also bases itself on traditional historical models is the 1977 London Central Mosque, perhaps better known as the Regent's Park Mosque, built to provide a focus and inspiration to the over half-million Muslims in the United Kingdom, which already has about five hundred mosques, of which about forty have been specifically constructed to serve as mosques.

In 1940 the Egyptian Ambassador to the Court of St James approached the Prime Minister, Neville Chamberlain, to purchase a site for a mosque as a reciprocal gesture to the Egyptian Government which had donated land in Cairo for the building of an Anglican cathedral some years earlier. The site at Hanover Gate in the park was formally obtained in 1944 by the Mosque Committee, which at that time was made up of twelve ambassadors from Muslim countries. The project was designed by an Egyptian architect, Ramzy Omar, but abandoned because of objections from the London County Council and the Fine Arts Commission. Finally, through an international design competition, a design by the British architect Sir Frederick Gibberd was selected. After modifications to the design, construction began in early 1974 at an estimated cost of £4.5 million donated by the Mosque Trust (Waqf) made up of a number of Muslim governments.

The triangular site in Regent's Park is almost entirely taken up by the mosque and cultural centre. The *qibla* wall, the most important element of the mosque, is pushed up to the edge of the site facing Mecca so that all other functions occur behind it. With the exception of the dome, which rises to a height of twenty-five metres (eighty feet), and the minaret, forty-three metres (140 feet) high, both of which function as important signs of the mosque's presence, the structure is built relatively low, nine-and-a-half metres (thirty feet), so as not to dominate the surrounding parkland and Nash's terrace just across the road. The layout of the facilities is linear in terms of the transition of spaces, from the courtyard to the entrance hall and from these to the prayer hall. The prayer hall for about a thousand people is rectangular, with the women's gallery (which represents about twenty per cent of the hall's floor area) recessed into the west wall. The hall is covered with a steel-framed dome, based on the form of the Iranian four-centred arch which is a repeated formal element in the building.

The London Central Mosque was designed to be an expression of an Islam that uses modern technologies and pan-Islamic design elements. The treatment of the arches, for instance, was that of their reinterpretation within modern technological language and concerned with the formal expression of contemporary building materials as developed by Rifat Chadirji and Mohamed Makiya in the early sixties.[10] However, the new technology, as expressed by the arches and modern materials, is somewhat inconsistent with the traditional forms of the minaret and dome.

In contrast to the preceding examples, the Mosque of Rome and the New York Islamic Cultural Center Mosque propose an architectural expression in a contemporary vein, and although they refer back to historical models, they both reinterpret traditional styles and principles in a modern idiom. The Mosque of Rome was substantially completed in 1992 and officially inaugurated in 1993. It offers a constructive solution to the problem of establishing a link with the past by evoking the historical model of the Great Mosque of Cordoba in terms of horizontality and the organic image of a forest of columns which the architects believe capture the atmosphere of spirituality in older mosques. In addition to the Moorish influence, Turkish and Persian styles are combined with Italian and specifically Roman imagery to reflect both the eclectic client and the *genus loci* of Rome.

Before the construction of the mosque, the international Muslim community had used rented premises for religious and cultural gatherings. In 1963 the Vatican Council agreed that it would allow the building of a mosque in Rome on condition that it was not in sight of St Peter's Basilica and that its minaret was no taller than the dome of St Peter's.[11] This cleared the way for the formation of the Centre in 1966. However, it was a visit to Italy in the early 1970s by the late King Faisal of Saudi Arabia that seems to have been the trigger for action to build the mosque. The design was the outcome of a 1975 competition where two projects, one by the Iraqi architect Sami Moussawi and the other by the Italian team of Paolo Portoghesi and Vittorio Gigliotti, were ultimately selected by a jury composed of professors from Islamic universities, Italian historians and a number of ambassadors to Italy from Muslim countries. The architects were asked to collaborate in a joint effort to produce a final design. A committee of thirteen ambassadors sponsored the project, twenty-four Muslim countries financed it, and the two-and-a-half hectare (six acre) site was donated by the Rome City Council in 1974. The design was approved, and work began in 1979, but unfortunately had to be interrupted due to insufficient funding. In 1984 the work recommenced with an infusion of funds from Saudi Arabia.

The complex is divided into two distinct parts: the prayer area and the library and cultural centre, separated by a colonnaded court. On the sloping site, the prayer hall is set against the mass of the Monte Antenne, while the rest of the construction is kept lower in order to maintain a harmonious relationship between the architecture and the natural environment. The landscape brings to mind Persian gardens, and the geometric layout with its horizontality of colonnades with their dynamic curves relate well to the site. The H-shaped complex creates continuously moving perspectives reminiscent of Michelangelo's Campidoglio in Rome and the inflected surfaces of Borromini's architecture.

The most successful element of the complex is the large prayer hall itself that accommodates over two thousand

Mosque of Rome, Italy

people and which combines the modular and circular systems of the classical Arab hypostyle hall and the central domed Ottoman model with its palm tree-like structure inspired by the mosque of Cordoba. The central dome and sixteen minor domes are supported by an intricate system of interwoven arches and columns reminiscent of the elegant mosque of Tlemcen. The seven-stepped central dome which measures almost twenty-four metres in diameter (seventy-eight feet), supported on eight columns, has mixed historical references in the cosmological image symbolising the Seven Heavens in the Prophet Mohammed's *Miraj Nama*, or Ascent to Heaven. The hall is lit naturally by glazed apertures in the domes, an effect that is replicated by the artificial lighting. The circular geometry of this project is a recurring theme in Portoghesi and Gigliotti's work, as can be seen in their projects for Amman and Khartoum, amongst others.

A woman's section, raised as a gallery covering some ten per cent of the prayer area, runs along the sides of the prayer hall, screened by carved lattice-work. The interior is decorated richly in *zellige*, mosaic work from Morocco. The tiles and the screens are executed with great delicacy and their rich traditional patterning and colours contrast strikingly with the monochrome interior and structure, as do the carpets. Using modern technology and materials, the architect's aim was to create an atmosphere of sacredness and solemnity, using, according to Portoghesi, 'the effects of lightness, dematerialisation and static paradox found in classical Islamic architecture' that would evoke the atmosphere of ancient mosques.[12] In this the architects have been successful in the prayer hall. Rather than make overt references to precise regional traditions or styles, the Mosque of Rome is a neutral expression of pan-Islamism in the sense that it attempts an architectural expression for all Muslims, regardless of their origins.

Similarly, the Islamic Cultural Center for New York uses easily recognisable elements associated with mosques to produce a modern building. The Centre, sponsored by the Islamic nations of the United Nations (UN), is located at 96th Street on New York's Upper East Side. Greater New York, which in the 1970s had no more than a dozen mosques, now has some 250 and by the mid 1980s there were over 600 mosques operating in the United States serving some three million Muslims.[13] The Muslims of New York form a wide ethnic and cultural mix – Lebanese, Pakistani, Yemeni and Turkish being predominant – and are the most highly educated in the Muslim *umma*.[14] It appears that an 'American Islam' may be emerging in the country – one which is distinguished by a general wish by Muslims living there to be seen as 'modern', be they liberal or conservative, and this holds true for the Muslim states represented at the UN.

It is therefore not surprising that the mosque, seen as a pan-Islamic symbol, is conceived both as a place of prayer and social exchange – a model that reflects diversity. The problem faced by the mosque committee of UN ambassadors was the same as the one in London, Washington DC and in Rome: namely, what should the building look like?

Like earlier mosques, the source of funding and decision-making was diverse, even though the Kuwaiti ambassador was a prime mover of the project, and the wish to be seen as being 'progressive' vis-a-vis the city and its non-Muslim inhabitants was imperatively in the mind of the building's sponsors. The building was first designed as a 'skyscraper mosque' in the 1970s; this proved to be too ambitious and the whole project was scaled down and put on hold. The project was re-launched in the 1980s and was given to the New York office of the firm Skidmore, Owings and Merrill (SOM) under the leadership of the project architect Michael McCarthy who was known to the client for his work in Kuwait. The architects were advised by two special committees of experts selected by the client to assist project definition. Unfortunately, the two committees had conflicting viewpoints: one urged the architect to follow literal historic motifs and the other encouraged total freedom of expression, with a respect for Muslim beliefs and architectural tradition. The architects chose to follow the latter although the client insisted that the Centre have a dome and a minaret.

The building, angled to the street grid because of orientation requirements, is based on a square grid and is itself essentially a vertically extended cube covered by a central dome. The design was modelled on the single-domed Ottoman mosque, proposed by the project architects, which included Mustafa Abadan, himself a Turk. The original idea remained, but it was revised and substantially reworked over time. The central space, which can house some one thousand worshippers, has a twenty-seven metre (ninety foot) clear span made up of four trusses supporting the steel and copper-clad concrete dome above, and suspending the women's mezzanine below. The mezzanine to the rear of the prayer hall covers an area about twenty per cent of that given to men. The whole space is carefully articulated and designed where the simplicity of monochromatic materials contrast with panels of blue tiles and greenish opaque glass in the upper areas of the hall, and with the striking blue *muqarnas mihrab* which is bordered by a frieze consisting of Qur'anic verses in Kufic. The main entrance portal also uses the same device of the glass *muqarnas*. Artificial lighting is provided by a circle of steel-wire supported lamps, a device dating to the suspended circles of oil lamps found at Ibn Tulun, Cairo, and elsewhere in Turkey. The corners and the top of the main structure are chamfered to emphasise the dome with its gilded crescent finial outside. The minaret, some forty metres (130 feet) tall, placed as a free-standing element, is a square shaft with an internal staircase with a balcony for the *muezzins* call to prayer – however, as with most new mosques, this is done by a recording transmitted through loudspeakers.

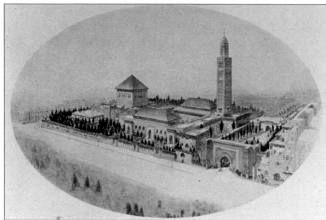

Also included within the structure are a conference hall and ablutions facilities. The first stage of the centre was completed and opened in 1991 and, although a second stage, including a library, classrooms and offices facilities was envisaged, no further work has yet been executed.

The illustrations are emblematic of trends in how Muslims present themselves to the outside world. As mentioned earlier, these expressions reflect a multi-cultural, multi-ethnic viewpoint, conceived through official state representation, as symbols of Islam in non-Muslim societies, and differ both in scale and programme from those mosques/centres built by local communities. In the case of the former, image is a primary concern and the presence of an international Muslim community is stressed. It is also generally apparent that in spite of the break with their home societies, the ambivalent attitude towards women in mosques remains – usually twenty per cent of the space is granted to them, despite them repre-senting a larger percentage of the population.

Mosque design in the West seems to have changed over the years: the earlier twentieth-century buildings were, in the main, more literal in their historicist expressions, whilst the later buildings from the 1980s onwards reveal a concern for projecting the 'modern Muslim'. However, tradition and modernity are seen as two sides of the same coin and the buildings reflect experiments in expressing the identity of populations acquiring new roots in the West. Interestingly, by contrast, buildings commissioned by national governments (as State mosques) and local authorities in Islamic countries appear to be increasingly more conservative and tradition-bound architecturally, referring to past models that are seen as manifestations of political and religious authority and legitimacy.[15]

There is a clear need to be able to deal simultaneously with an overlay of aspirations and material conditions. The simultaneous reality of global and local cultures is upon us. It is with reference to these that the multiplicities of actualities are now merely parts of the same web in which we all find ourselves, and with which we must deal. Nineteenth-century nationalism established what we might call the modern ground rule for having an identity – you have the strongest identity when you are least aware of yourself. Twentieth-century realities of pan-national multi-culturalism and multi-national economic forces with global communications are also bringing with them the expression of a lowest common denominator, understood by individuals and nation states.

These building expressions of Muslim communities in transition raise wider issues about cultural assimilation. The architecture of the mosques provides one set of clues to understanding the needs of recent Muslim migrants – foreigners in a foreign land – in societies of cultural diversity and ever-increasing immigration. If public buildings and spaces are to reflect the multi- and inter-cultural realities of today's societies, the many fragmented boundaries that are created by a diversity of populations need to find a voice and a place. The 'other' needs not only to be recognised as such, but should also be considered an important participant in the formation of a 'new world order'. How Muslims view and express themselves within such contexts becomes important for cross-cultural understanding and development. The current message that seems to be transmitted by the mosque in the West is: we have our own identity and yet we wish to be part of the society into which we have entered, but we are not yet part of this world we inhabit because we are still unsure of ourselves and of our place within it.

NOTES

1 For a recent account and analysis see Robin Wright, 'Islam, Democracy and the West', *Foreign Affairs*, Vol 71, No 3, Summer 1992, p145. The term 'Islamist' is used here to describe interpretive and sometimes forward-looking and innovative attempts to reconstruct the social order within the religious traditions of Islam. As Wright has pointed out, the various Islamic movements are often called 'fundamentalist' in the West, but most are in fact not so in their agendas. Fundamentalism generally urges adherence to literal reading of the religious texts and does not advocate change in the social order, instead focuses on reforming the lives of the individual and family. Most of today's Islamic movements resemble Catholic Liberation theologians who urge active use of original religious doctrine to better the temporal and political lives in a modern world.

2 Gregory Bateson (1970) argues that people focus on perceived differences as a way to make sense of the world and this, in fact, gives shape and form to the societies and permits cultural labelling and classification.

3 I am indebted to Richard Sennett who has written about these ideas in his seminal works and in an unpublished paper entitled *The Foreigner*, presented at the Urban Forum conference on 'Ethnicity, Migration and the City', in New York, October 1980. He and I differ on interpretation, but I agree with his broad-brush characterisation of changes in people brought about by displacement from their societal roots.

4 Note my emphasis on shifting intellectual paradigms. The realities are somewhat different where, I believe, we are witnessing the dramatic and bloody death throes of both nationalist and ethnic assertions of identity, as in Eastern Europe and Central Asia.

5 This issue of 'boundaries' has been discussed in unpublished presentations: *Dissolving/Resolving Boundaries: Difference and Differentiation in Disciplines, Cultures and Practices* by Setha M Low and mine, *Displacing/Replacing Boundaries: Expressions of 'the Other' in Architecture*, at the Built Form and Culture Research Conference held in Cincinnati, October 1993. In her paper Low calls for the dissolving/resolving of boundaries within a post-modern construct. However, I do not believe that this will be possible in the foreseeable future – but the idea is a nice one.

6 'America and Alfred Stieglitz', *Selected Essays of William Carlos Williams*, New Directions Paperbacks, New York, 1969, p134.

7 This view of cultural distinctiveness is borne out by several studies: see Dr Mazammil H Siddiqui, 'Muslims in a Non-Muslim Society', *Brighton Islamic Centre Bulletin*, Vol 15, No 3, July-September 1991. Also, Akbar S Ahmed's discussions of Muslims as minorities in his general interest book (based on the television series) *Living Islam*, BBC Books, London.

8 Information on the mosques is taken from a forthcoming book, *Contemporary Mosques* by Renata Holod and myself – a study undertaken over six years of some eighty case studies based on original research, and other examples brought to our attention, notably by the Aga Khan Award for Architecture.

9 For a history of the Centre, see Dr Muhammad Abdul-Rauf, *History of the Islamic Centre*, The Washington DC Islamic Center, 1978.

10 Makiya and Chadirji, two prominent architects working throughout the Middle East, were very influential through their use of materials – such as concrete and steel – in simplified arch forms in their projects which were seen as new reinterpretations of Islamic architecture. They have been copied and extensively repeated for almost two decades.

11 According to an essay in the *Middle East Economic Digest*, 25-31 July 1989, p22. However, the architect believes that the only real obstacle to the height of the minaret was the restriction imposed by the Municipal building code.

12 Paolo Portoghese, 'Elogio Della Contamazione', *XX Secolo*, 1992, pp4-11, gives a good explanation of the architect's view.

13 'View from a Jersey City Mosque', *The New Yorker*, September 27, 1993, p31.

14 For a study of Islam in the United States, see Yvonne Haddad and Adair Lumis's, *Islamic Values in the United States*, Oxford University Press, New York, 1987. The information herein is taken from this published study of 1983, which still remains essentially correct, ten years after it was undertaken.

15 The issue of legitimacy and authenticity in the architecture of the Islamic world is one that is currently of great debate and concern by scholars concerned with Islam, modernity and its cultural expressions. The historian Mohamed Arkoun has argued repeatedly that contemporary Muslim governments resort to the use of historically-accepted styles of architecture to reinforce an image of longevity, permanence and legitimacy. Such architecture is viewed as having the weight of authenticity. For a discussion on authenticity, see Hasan-Uddin Khan, 'Meaning in Tradition Today: An Approach to Architectural Criticism' and 'Counterpoint' by Michael Sorkina, both in *Criticism in Architecture*, Aga Khan Award for Architecture, Geneva, 1989, pp53-69. For a more detailed discussion of issues of legitimacy and Islam facing Modernity see Arkoun, *Overtures sur l'Islam* (2nd ed), Paris, 1992.

AKAA, 1986, rehabilitation of ksour, Draa Valley

REHABILITATION OF KSOUR, DRAA VALLEY, MOROCCO

Jamel Akbar

So many projects have been nominated for the Aga Khan Award that quite a number of them have reached the final stages of screening and been reviewed by the technical reviewers. A few of them won the Award and thus received attention through publicity. However, those which did not make it did not enjoy such attention, although there is much to learn from them. This is one of the hidden assets of the Aga Khan Award.

The Aga Khan Award is building a library of technical reports with full documentation of important projects that did not have the chance of winning. When those materials become accessible, they will be a valuable source of education for both professionals and academicians. This paper will give one example of an excellent project that was nominated and reviewed twice but failed to win.

In 1986 Mr Raol Snelder was the Technical Reviewer for the rehabilitation of ksour, a job which I inherited in 1989. I had the opportunity to learn a tremendous amount from reviewing the project. This case stands as a good representational example of the many excellent projects that are not yet known to professionals.

The ksour (plural of ksar) are compact fortified villages which are closely built on the edge of the oasis-like river beds, against inhospitable and barren mountainous backgrounds. The ksour are built of mud and are lived in by a sedentary farming population. The compact fabric has an urban appearance that is marked by *burjs* (towers). The fundamental problem with the ksour was that the outstanding traditional mud architecture was decaying through lack of maintenance, which in turn was caused by a tendency of exodus.

More than twenty-five years ago Monsieur Jean Hensens, with the assistance of Moroccan technicians, studied and proposed the 'Draa Valley Project'. The concept of the project was self-help, taking advantage of the tradition building skills of the local population that was largely under-employed, to preserve the dwindling heritage of traditional mud architecture. The project did not aim to take care of all problems; its strategy was to provide an impetus which might help stop the exodus which was decaying the ksour. To preserve the physical form, there was minimum intervention, which meant maximum participation, and this was a shortcut for a higher quality environment. Nevertheless, there are many inevitable problems that are beyond all involved individuals' control – such as drought. For a passerby, the project may not appear to be as successful as it is. The residents' poverty camouflages reality. A comparison between those ksour that were renovated by the project and the ones that were not, and the sharp contrast between their physical quality and their residents' condition, reveals the initiators' originality, especially if one considers that the project commenced only twenty-five years ago.

The Ksour and their Site

Although the climate is harsh during summer, where the average maximum temperature is over 30°C for seven months and reaches 44°C in July, with the average minimum of 10°C during four to five months of winter and reaching as low as 3°C in January, the ksour managed to respond to this harsh climate. The *iksar* houses offer an excellent environment during most parts of the year. The residents proudly argue that the temperature remains constant during all the seasons, as streets are continuously ventilated by a cool flow of air. However, diurnal variation – as a monthly average – is rarely less than 15°C or more than 18°C which means that traditional houses offer a good environment during most of the year. Hot winds charging the air with dust and sand are not unusual.

Annual rainfall declines as one descends into the pre-Saharian region, coming from Marrakesh through the Atlas Mountains. Some years there is hardly any rain at all, thus rain-dependent agriculture is not possible.

The south-east side of the Anti-Atlas is a desert that accommodates some fertile valleys such as the Draa Valley (Wadi Dar'a), the Gheris, the Dades and the Ziz. The melted snow creates a linear oasis river bed in which water is used for irrigation for most parts of the year. The Draa River reaches its mouth (Mhamid) only in years of comparatively heavy rainfall. The seventeen renovated ksour are located between the towns of Agdz and Zagora (land area of ninety-four kilometres) where the site is fairly flat and the valley drifts towards a backdrop of distant mountains.

If the relief of the Draa Valley is shallow, the ksour will dominate the surrounding environment as they are located on high ground. The existing approach is from the main road where the lack of vegetation contrasts sharply with

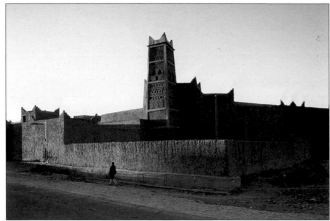

Rehabilitation of ksour, Draa Valley, 1986

the traditional original entrance from the green oasis. Some ksour lie on the edge, or in the middle of the oasis. Most ksour in the Draa Valley can be easily reached from the main road between Ouarzazate and Zagora (162 kilometres) which runs along the edge of the oasis.

The original ksour form is open to many theoretical speculations. One of the most likely explanations is that they came with the Arab and Arabised Berber tribes (for example, the Beni Hilal who arrived in the twelfth century, the majority of whom crossed the Atlas Mountains while a few remained in the valleys; the Beni Ma'qul who came between the thirteenth and fourteenth centuries, some of whom currently live in Zagora and Asrir; and the Beni Hassan who have mostly remained in the desert). Supporting this theory are the many Arabic names of the ksour. This hypothesis may also explain the similarity between the Yemeni architecture and the ksour. Another functional explanation is that nomads and sedentaries have lived for centuries in intimate but sometimes antagonistic and interdependent relationships, which may have given the ksour their present form.

There are no clear patterns to the streets of the ksour. However, the narrow streets are sometimes laid out according to a grid-like pattern or with a few dead end streets connecting the main streets. The most interesting architectural feature is the lighting inside the ksour. Streets are often covered with long overpasses or *sabats*, creating narrow, dim streets and sometimes totally dark dead end streets. The reason, they say, is that flies usually avoid darkness. With dates (which are sweet) being the main source of food, and the hot climate, the inside of the ksour is the only place for flies to retreat to. To solve this, the residents maximise dark spaces. The ksour's darkness and the residents' ability to control light within houses and public spaces against the bright desert light is perhaps the most innovative feature of this type of architecture. Sometimes the lights in the streets in between the *sabats* are like spot lights in a tunnel, while the light of the courtyard inside the houses is like a spotlight in a cave.

Burjs mark the ksour's defensive walls. They are placed regularly on the outer wall or on the houses of the wealthy. Each tower can have a different decorative style and they are usually extensions of staircases.

The typical house is usually a two-storey building which is constructed on 150 to 250 square metres. Houses of the well-to-do can be of three-storeys (but rarely more), with the top floor doubling-up as a roof terrace. Here there are a few other rooms which serve as bedrooms. Doors between roof parapets allow the residents to move from one house to another, especially the case amongst houses of close relatives.

Long narrow rooms are arranged around the central square or rectangular open space, in which four to eight thick square- or L-shaped columns surround a central courtyard. Sometimes there are no walls between spaces around the courtyard, thus forming one large space with the columns in the centre marking the light well. The court is usually walled by a less than one metre high parapet above the roof terrace which receives a modicum of light controlled by the placing of mats on the opening.

Users

Hensens put the number of ksour-dwellers in the Draa Valley in 1971 at 124,000 living in 350 ksour of diverse sizes; while the number of the people who benefited directly from the project amounting to approximately 20,000 to 25,000 (or about 18% of the total initial target population). The population of one of the ksour that benefitted from the project (Asrir) is 1,500-1,800. The majority of current users are farmers in the low to very low income category. The economy was delicately balanced in the past and was based on farming. The oasis dwellers grow barley, sorghum, wheat, vegetables, olive trees and some other fruits, the most important being date palm. Dates are very important for the economy. A family in ksar Asrir could own anything from 100 to 200 palm trees. One tree would give up to 100 kilogrammes/year of dates. The highest quality date is usually sold for 10 DH/ kilogrammes (in 1988), the middle quality (worth 7 DH/ kilogrammes) is stored and consumed by the inhabitants and the lowest is fed to the animals. The leaves and the wood of palm trees are used for building materials, flat dishes, deep baskets and firewood. Livestock consists of cows, donkeys, sheep, goats and chickens.

The Problem

The Moroccan five-year (1968-1972) development plan combined the policy of agricultural development with an agricultural investment code and a plan for important hydraulic projects. The regions affected by this were to experience changes from a subsistence oriented production to an industrialised commercial agriculture. The plan was that with increased revenues in those rural areas, modernisation of the rural habitat would stimulate production and create employment, thus reducing a rural exodus to towns. A programme to construct 60,000 new houses throughout Morocco was included. The restoration and renovation of 30,000 houses in the ksour valleys were included in the five year programme. Assistance was requested from the World Food Program (WFP) in rural housing developed schemes, in the hope that this would improve the living conditions of the farmers affected by agrarian reform, and the redistribution of land in the areas earmarked for development.

Although the oasis in the region is known to be the richest in water in North Africa, the prolonged droughts and the new ecological conditions created by the dam near Quarzazate, and a palm tree disease combined with the population growth and the increased number of settling nomads have all affected the local economy.

The migration of the wealthy to cities leaving their farms to be exploited by farmers (*khammas* or *rabba'*) on rent contracts who may not care about the properties as owners do, and the out-migration of craftsmen whose skills are better rewarded elsewhere, are other major factors that affected the economy negatively. Thus, it can be said that the region is not sufficiently equipped to support the growing population. Compared to the cities, the majority of the population living in the ksour live at a substandard level. The poorest living in a city can at least re-use an old piece of furniture, but in the ksour even this privilege is denied. Most houses have no furniture other than dishes and a mat. The new influences on the Draa Valley societies and the strain on the traditional delicately balanced economy affected the socio-cultural situation to such an extent that it resulted in migration – this area is thought to have the highest migration rate in Morocco.

Since the mid 1970s government expenditure has increased in the region. The reason is purely political as the government hopes this will re-establish Morocco's authority over the former Spanish Sahara. Major towns like Quarzazate and Zagora experienced considerable change during the seventies, however, with little impact on the ksour populations. For example, the large new Hotel-Club Reda Zagora (with over three hundred beds) was built recently in the town of Zagora – none of the local labour force, it seems, was used in its construction.

A Solution

A group of architects who had gained experience in traditional mud construction in Marrakesh in previous years, created a favourable climate for the Draa Valley Project and it is said to have been a factor in the creation of the CERF (Centre d'Experimentation, de Recherche et de Formation). The Minister, as well as top level civil servant gave considerable freedom to the architects and other personnel of the CERF for the project's formulation.

During the first phase some pilot studies and experimental projects were carried out. The ksour were carefully analysed and the necessary materials and expenses of labour for rehabilitation and upgrading were identified for each ksar, in consultation with the local authorities. Even the needs of individual houses, such as private water-wells, and the needs of the community, such as collective stables and public buildings, were estimated. Those proposals were then discussed with the villagers concerned, and accordingly a final plan was prepared for each ksar. The responsibility of implementing the plan in the seventeen ksour in the Draa Valley was delegated to the Marrakesh regional delegation of the Direction de l'Urbanisme et de l'Habitat (1971-75).

The three general objectives were: the rehabilitation of the ksour in the Draa Valley, in order to maintain and upgrade valuable housing stock and to create a unique habitat with considerable potential for the tourist industry;

Rehabilitation of ksour, Draa Valley, 1986

Rehabilitation of ksour, Draa Valley, 1986

to plan for future harmonious extensions of the ksour; and to reduce under-employment and rural exodus.

The WFP were closely connected to the main objectives this project was trying to implement. The majority of the project's beneficiaries were rural low-income households, the group the WFP is meant to help in the first place; the self-help approach and creation of jobs for the under-employed population fitted the WFP guidelines; and the agricultural development projects being carried out at the same time as the project could qualify as an early example of the integrated development approach.

Implementation

The local population carried out the work as an assisted self-help project, as well as a small enterprise. Skilled labourers or builders (*mu'llimin*) were paid 7DH (in 1989, US$1 = 8.24DH) and one food ration a day. Unskilled workers (*khuddam*) were paid only one daily ration which was: 400 grammes of wheat or wheat flour; 20 grammes of condensed or dried milk; 30 grammes of vegetable oil; 20 grammes of sugar; and 2 grammes of tea. Builders who participated in the project say that the value of one ration when sold was almost half the daily paid wage, ie: 3.5DH.

The project aimed to improve hygienic conditions. For example, stables were built outside the ksar for the cattle, who were traditionally brought into the houses. It also aimed to enhance the quality of the public domain by paving streets and private properties, and rebuilding ruined houses or renovating those in need of mainte-nance. The functional requirements were to initiate, prepare and monitor the renovation of ksar houses in order to upgrade the quality of the built environment. In this process, maximum use has to be made of local manpower and local materials. Public spaces and commu-nal buildings were to be maintained; functional require-ments were to be modified in order to create a more sanitary environment, such as reusing ground floors that functioned traditionally as stables and latrines; and water supply was also to be improved.

The original five-year plan of building 60,000 tradi-tional houses and renovating 30,000 dwellings, requiring a total of 150 million individual food rations, was reduced to 28,700 units. The renovation in the villages was reduced to 4,530 units. Furthermore, the total of 4,374 units representing 69.5% of the target have been covered in the ksour (seventeen ksar in the Draa Valley and three in Ziz).

The infrastructure works serving the twenty ksour included: building thirteen mosques, three Qu'ran schools, 583 stables and 212 septic tanks; creating fifteen gateways; digging nineteen wells; reconstructing 455,000 square metres of side walls and 1,500 meters of water courses for supply and irrigation; and paving 95,000 square metres of streets and public squares.

However, the fact remains that the ksour need constant

maintenance and the notion that they are no longer the answer to people's aspirations are inevitable questions. The gap between the inhabitants' contemporary requirements and the degree to which the ksour provide satisfaction is indeed the major problem in this type of project. Nonetheless, the gap is relative, depending on the family's wealth. In a few cases the ksar is deserted or left to farmworkers (*khammasin* and *rabba'in*); in other cases the ksar is kept as a secondary residence or a reception house for visitors.

The project also fell prey to some miscalculation: although it aimed to stable livestock outside the ksour, some users still brought their livestock into the houses, claiming that the outside stables were not sufficient in number. The users also connected a number of stables by knocking down walls to form one large one. Furthermore, although the project provided communal water wells with pumps, some wells were not used; this meant that either the wells were misplaced or caused conflict among users and were thus abandoned. When streets were paved, some of the house levels remained lower than street level. No matter what, such problems are inevitable.

I have entered many buildings which had not been maintained for a long time (in one case sixty years) and their interiors were still in a good condition! The main problem of mud as a building material is its susceptibility to rainwater and thus its need for frequent exterior maintenance. Some of the renovated houses in this project (thirteen years ago) do need a little maintenance. In this respect, considering rainfall in the region (less than 100 millimetres), one may argue that rather than using other building materials which will need less frequent maintenance but cost more, one should continue using the mud technique to invest in future employment, unless an affordable breakthrough in technology is found.

Achievement of Objectives
Users are definitely optimistic. The sharp contrast in terms of quality between the renovated ksour and the ones that are not, tells the whole story. Those who live in the renovated ksour are interested in maintaining their properties. Those living in the ones that are not, are reluctant to invest in their properties because of the deteriorated public spaces. According to Raol Snelder (p15 of the report), 'the project's physical achievements are well integrated in the traditional environment and an effort has been made to allow for the inevitable change in the attitudes, the needs and the aspirations of the users. Renovation work has been carried out in a sensitive way in a unique habitat'.

The project's achievements have stimulated pride in the beneficiaries and in ownership amongst the residents. Therefore, one of the major objectives of the project – establishing a working relationship with the communities involved – has been achieved. Interviewed users' responses have been pleasingly positive.

One of the project's objectives was to maintain traditional craft in the region by employing a considerable number of craftsmen. This objective was accomplished for a certain period, but craftsmen (especially the younger ones), who had a chance of making a better income in richer regions, are steadily leaving the valley, a trend this project cannot stop.

When the project was initiated in 1968 it was certainly an original concept and it still is for many decision makers of the Third World countries. The principles of rehabilitation through maximum utilisation of local resources led to minimum external intervention. Minimum external intervention obviously means maximum local participation, a shortcut for high quality environments.

This paper was developed from a technical review report submitted to the Aga Khan Award in 1989, based on a one week site visit to the Draa Valley and on documents provided by the Aga Khan Award for Architecture. Among these are the Technical Review Report of Roal Snelder and some Moroccan and WFP official documents.

Swabili Housing

THE ARCHEOLOGICAL AND ARCHITECTURAL HERITAGE OF EAST AFRICA

Omar Bwana

Historical scientists are fascinated by the East Africa Coast which is home to a number of important urban sites associated with the Islamic Cultural Heritage. A complex interdependent Swahili society has developed over the past two thousand years with cosmopolitan commercial towns, settled merchants and craftsmen from all around the Indian Ocean circle and South-East Asia. Islamic waves in the East African Coast started in the eighth century AD and by the early tenth century, when Al-Musud, an Arab historian visited some islands off the coast, Islamic settlements had been well established. The earliest substantiation of this history is found in a Kufic inscription dated 500/1107 AD in the mosque of Kiskimkazi, Zanzibar.

Archeological evidence is now emerging which is relevant to this historical debate and we are able to supplement knowledge from historical sources with it. Currently, the earliest coast settlements to have been discovered date from the eighth, ninth and tenth centuries. The most important Islamic towns of this early period, at which excavations have been made, are Shanga and Manda in Kenya, and Kilwa in Tanzania. Further research and survey has identified some four hundred sites on the East Africa Coast, many of which contain a stone structure in the form of a mosque, houses or tombs. Some are of sufficient size and importance to be described as towns.

Kenya has placed considerable emphasis on preserving her cultural heritage by the support of paleontological and archeological research into the origin of man. It is equally important to preserve evidence of our most recent past, because, in reconstructing history we gain greater insight into the dynamics of cultural change. There is no point in disputing whether to preserve or abandon something on the basis of material allegedly classified as being either 'indigenous' or 'nonindigneous'. All that man has created in our land is of equal importance in our cultural heritage.

The National Museum of Kenya – following government policy – has taken several steps to ensure the satisfactory preservation and conservation of these historical towns and sites. More, it should be noted, has been done in the last decade than in the previous five decades. Making an inventory of all sites and monuments along the Kenyan coast has been an on-going process. The National Museum of Kenya has already produced two volumes of monographs, *The Monumental Architecture* and *Archeology of the Kenya Coast*. Along the Kenya coast alone, there are over 120 ancient towns and settlements. These settlements are of a stone structure and have impressive architectural features. They fall into five categories:

1 Unoccupied sites of ruined houses, mosques and tombs.
2 Unoccupied sites covering ruined townships, fortified areas and enclosures.
3 Remains of past habitations in areas still partly occupied.
4 Urban areas of historic and architectural importance.
5 Monuments in established towns or villages.

All of these cities and monuments are protected by law under the Antiquities and Monuments Act.

In recognition of the importance of preserving historical towns and sites along the Kenya coast, the Government, through the National Museum of Kenya, has embarked on a policy of conservation of Lamu Town and Mombasa. In 1975, the National Museum of Kenya and the Ministry of Lands and Settlements sponsored a detailed study, *Lamu: A Study in Conservation* by Usam Ghaidan, of Lamu's old town and the antiquities of Lamu district, with the objective of fostering conservation and sensitive development. In 1983, the National Museum of Kenya with the assistance of UNESCO, again launched the Lamu conservation project. The result of this event was the book *Planning Lamu* by Francesco Siravo and Ann Pulver, which outlined the present conditions of the town and introduced the policy necessary for responsible conservation and development. As a direct result of the successful work carried out in Lamu, the National Museum of Kenya decided to expand its effort to include a programme for conservation of the old town Mombasa, to be funded by the United Nations Development Programme (UNDP), with technical aid coming from UNESCO.

It is the responsibility of the National Museum of Kenya, as custodian of Historical Sites and Monuments, to ensure that these sites are researched, preserved and conserved, and presented to the public. The historical, archeological and architectural heritage of East Africa is a fragile, non-renewable resource which requires integrated policies of protection and active participation by the general public in order to avoid future destruction.

Swahili Housing

Swahili Housing

FROM ABOVE, L to R: AKAA, 1992, Kampung Kali Cho-De, Yogyakarta, Indonesia; Kampung Kali Cho-De, Yogyakarta, Indonesia; AKAA, 1986, Honourable Mention, Ismaïliyya Development Project, Egypt; AKAA, 1980, Kampung Improvement Programme, Jakarta, Indonesia

THE SOCIAL CHALLENGE TO MODERN ISLAMIC ARCHITECTURE

SOEDJATMOKO

Meeting in these beautiful and historic surroundings, it is unfortunately impossible not to be acutely aware of the sounds of war close by and the cries of human suffering. It forcefully reminds us of the extent to which we are part of, and affected by, the very profound changes which are now taking place in the patterns of the global distribution of power and the continuing fragmentation of world-wide and regional alignments which is a result of the projection of heightened economic and political competition on different parts of the world in a situation of nuclear stalemate. Its impact on an increasingly malfunctioning international economic system is further aggravated by the fares engendered by the inevitable vulnerabilities of all societies, large and small, strong and weak, in this increasingly crowded, interdependent, complex and fragile world.

We are equally affected by the profound and continuing social changes which result from changing value perceptions and aspirations of people as distinct from governments in both the industrial and developing world, for example, the environmental, human rights, women's and peace movements. These are all manifestations of that almost autonomous process that began with the liberation movements of the Third World towards national independence after World War II.

In addition, there is also the process of internal fragmentation which results from profound and rapid social and psychological change affecting aspirations and behaviour of groups of people, hitherto socially and politically ineffective; people at the bottom of our societies in both the industrial and the developing world. These changes upset existing social, and sometimes even political balances.

It is, however, also possible to sense, through the din of war, the agony of conflict even amongst ourselves, and the swirling cross-currents of change, the search for new patterns of purpose and cohesiveness reversing the earlier process of stagnation and decay, and for the social and political arrangements that make this possible. One can observe a new assertiveness of the cultures which had for a long period been marginalised and powerless. This includes what is often called the resurgence of Islam in its various forms. Indeed, we may be at the painful beginnings of a long historical process, leading to the re-emergence of a modern Islamic civilisation, together with other non-Western industrial civilisations, on the basis of equality in a pluralistic world.

Whether these impulses will be able to carry us through such a process of self-renewal from within our own societies and carry us out of the deep crisis in which we find ourselves, will to a large extent depend on whether the culture of Islam will be capable of giving an effective Islamic response to the problems besetting our societies: massive endemic poverty; large and rapidly increasing populations; and inequitable social structures. This in turn will depend not on whether Islamic culture can adjust to the dynamics of science and technology, but rather on whether our cultures will be able to harness, redirect and develop science and technology for the modernisation and self-renewal of our cultures within the context of the transcendental conception of life which is the essence of Islamic culture.

Seen from this perspective, it is quite likely that the patterns of development and the trajectory of industrialisation in those low-income Islamic countries with large populations will be different from those of the industrialised nations of the West. The necessity to develop our countries from a broad social basis, rather than through the expansion of the modern sector of former colonial or dependent societies, and to involve large populations in a dynamic revitalisation of the countryside where most of the people live, as well as the crowded informal sectors of the urban centres, is bound to lead to different patterns of spatial organisation, urban-rural configurations, and transportation flows. These human settlement requirements, reinforced by the high costs of energy, pose new architectural problems, the solution to which may well influence the physical shape, quality and style of modern Islamic civilisation.

We are all very much aware that we are the inheritors of a great architectural tradition, reflecting in the variety of its architectural idioms the richness of grandeur of past Islamic civilisation. At the same time, we are also fully aware that we can no longer automatically draw from that tradition in our efforts to respond to these new challenges and needs, because of the sharp and traumatic discontinuities which characterise our recent past and our present solution. We are, in fact, just beginning to find ourselves

AKAA, 1992, Kampung Kali Cho-De, Yogyakarta, Indonesia

AKAA, 1992, Kampung Kali Cho-De, Yogyakarta, Indonesia

after the collapse of colonial rule and foreign domination with its confusion of architectural styles imposed on the traditions of our societies.

As in all cultures recovering from foreign domination, the alienation from one's own cultural identity has been accompanied by a considerable loss of style and taste, a loss which is reflected in the architectural features of our cities, and which after independence, was only further aggravated by the stylistic confusion of modern cosmopolitan architecture. This is one reason why we will not be able to draw creatively from our great cultural heritage until Islamic culture has recaptured its essential core and authenticity and, as a result, recaptures its self-confidence.

There is a second reason why we cannot do so. The nature and the scale of urgency of the social situation in which we now find ourselves is so different from anything in the history of Islamic civilisation, that it suggests the likelihood that modern Islamic architecture may have to pose to itself anew the most elementary questions. We must reconsider the definition of architectural needs, relating quantity, volume, costs, quality and content to the problems of poverty, demography and justice, as well as its function and role in design and conception, before it can begin to discover the possibly new relevance to our present and future needs, hidden in the architectural richness of our past.

These reflections suggest two outcomes. Firstly, that the responses to the extremely varied social, economic, political and ecological conditions and the different cultural and architectural history in the many nations of Islam, may lead to an even greater variety of architectural styles. In light of the demographic distribution, this is just as likely to be determined by the hundreds of millions of Muslims in Asia and Africa with their own architectural traditions, with often strong, pre-Islamic roots, as those in the Middle Eastern and Arab world.

Secondly, it seems rather unlikely that a new Islamic architectural style will develop from adaptations of modern cosmopolitan architecture or from adaptations of Islamic monumental tradition.

Inevitably, buildings will continue to be built, but at the same time, Islamic architectural self-renewal is more likely to come from the wrestling of architects, city and national planners, and of our societies as a whole. It is in the problems of housing the poor and the many that the vernacular Islamic tradition may prove to be of more direct relevance.

No architect working in the Islamic world can afford to leave these speculations aside for the moment, or to ignore these questions. He cannot afford to think only in terms of single buildings or complexes. Except in a few cases, he will have to think totally of the human environment within the resource constraints prevailing in low-income countries which suffered from the impact of high energy costs. He will have to work with urban and na-

tional planners in the context of a search for alternative energy-conserving strategies and spatial organisation of human activities.

He will have to develop urban communities with materials and methods that are not energy-intensive, and settlement patterns that bring housing, employment place and commercial and production centres to human scale. The communities must be within walking distance of the centres of worship which in the past have been so instrumental in determining the rhythm in Islamic cities.

The challenges facing the architect in Islamic countries also stem from the rapid increase in population. He cannot but realise that during the lifetime of the major buildings and complexes he will design, the population of the country in which he works may double with many consequences for his buildings.

In addition, his architectural response to the needs of housing the poor will have to adapt to the growing realisation that poverty cannot be overcome merely by the provision of services and assistance to the poor and the socially weak. This can only by accomplished with their active and voluntary participation, utilising the means provided to them, as well as by the enhancement of their social effectiveness through self-organisation and self-management. If Barbara Ward's observation is correct, as I believe it is, that very few housing projects for the poor have really been utilised by the poor, and that it is very likely impossible for one class of society to build houses for another class lower on the social ladder, then the role of the architect in our Islamic societies, as well as his training will require considerable redefinition.

His training, then should also sensitise him to the implication of the fact that most of the poor, and most of the people in society, live in the countryside. Their development needs and efforts in a situation of high energy cost and rapid population increase pose new problems asking for new architectural solutions. Very few of the university-trained architects in the Third World have cared to address these problems. Neither have they, generally speaking, cared to involve themselves in the search of the poor towards more satisfactory solutions or to the shelters, dwellings and improvements they have built for themselves in their new or old urban settlements.

The poor, large, densely packed, rapidly increasing populations and their housing needs in the high-energy cost situations are not the only social challenges which modern Islamic architecture will have to face as we move into the twenty-first century. Profound and often rapid shifts in perceptions of values, some of which I have referred to earlier, are taking place which are bound to affect the demands put on architects and architecture in Islamic countries. I will mention only a few as examples. The concept of interiors, for instance, which has been so characteristic of traditional Middle Eastern architecture is bound to be affected by changing lifestyles, by changes in the role of women, and also by changing perception and needs that govern the balance between the commercial, professional, and organised public activities and the non-commercial community and family-oriented, status- and culture-enhancing activities of each of our societies. Modern communications are, in addition, bound to have an impact on social mobility, on conceptions of privacy, accessibility and the architectural expression of the differentiation between exterior and interior space.

In responding to the massive need for low-cost housing within the constraints of low-income economics and high-energy costs, the architect, as well as his client, will have to address the question of breaking up the traditional extended three-generation family into nuclear, two-generation families. No architect or planner can ignore the profound social, cultural and economic consequences of that decision in terms of family stability and the care for the aged, children and the disabled.

As to governmental architecture, the relationship between government and the governed in our countries is also in a process of profound change. As a result of improving access to education, there is a higher level of political consciousness and social effectiveness in large numbers of people emerging from traditional situations of powerlessness and passivity. Also, the likelihood of the population doubling, coupled with modern communications technology, is bound to have an important impact on administrative, bureaucratic and political processes and structures, with significant consequences for the design, location and dispersal of government buildings, as well as for their relationship to the public at large.

Likewise, no educational planner or architect in our Islamic countries could ignore the impact of modern communications technology on the design and location of the institutes of higher education. Electronic technology may soon make classrooms obsolete, devoting itself to the scientific ethos and discipline. Such development would turn expensive university buildings, designed to house large numbers of students at a safe distance from over-crowded population centres, into white elephants, even within the effective life of the buildings. Such a develop-ment might also reduce the danger that the physical and social isolation from society at large university complexes would produce either arrogant technocrats of narrow ideologists, both equally sensitive to, and ignorant of, the real problems of the society they are expected to be able to help solve.

Having made these few, primarily illustrative remarks on the social environment that will determine the func-tions to which Islamic urban and rural population centres should be able to respond, it is also important to state that these remarks and the possible architectural solutions to these problems are essential, but not necessarily sufficient conditions for the development of a modern distinctive architectural style.

Looking at the great architectural styles in human history one comes to realise the extent to which great architecture has been the product of great faith – not of a single individual, but of a whole society. That faith may be religious, as is the case with most historical styles, but it may also be secular, as demonstrated by the works of the great modern Western architects early this century. Their style reflected the almost unlimited faith in man's capacity to shape his own environment and control his own destiny. Such secular faith has, in recent decades, been on the wane, and much of contemporary architecture is rather a reflection of superficial fashions on individual idiosyn-crasies of architect or client. However, what we are now witnessing in many cultures all over the world is a resur-gence of religion, which may be what a noted sociologist has called the 'return of the sacred'.

It seems obvious that in our societies only a major resurgence of faith may eventually take the struggle for the right architectural solutions or responses to the massive and urgent social challenges of our times – poverty, population and injustice – to the level where a great new Islamic architectural style could gradually emerge. This would put the architect close to the centre of the traditional Islamic striving for a just and moral society that is also democratic.

It is to an important extent his creativity and social responsibility, as well as the creative architectural proc-esses he is capable of inspiring among the so-called common people and the bureaucracy that may trigger the articulation and physical image of Islam as a design for the future. In that process it can be hoped that the architec-ture produced may become the markers on the road to a new social and political spirituality that will be the heart of a revitalised, dynamic, modern Islamic civilisation.

This is an edited version of a speech given by the late Dr Soedjatmoko, then Rector of the United Nations University (Tokyo) at a seminar during the Awards presentation ceremonies in Lahore, Pakistan in October 1980.

THE AGA KHAN AWARD FOR ARCHITECTURE

Suha Özkan

During the 1960s and 70s, the deterioration of the built environment and disfigurement of the architectural heritage in Muslim lands proceeded at an ever-increasing pace, exacerbated by rampant population growth and the introduction of new, imported technologies, with little promise for amelioration in the future. Within this context, His Highness the Aga Khan shared the concern and commitment of many others to try to halt this process, and determined to find the means of encouraging a resurgence of the building arts which had always characterised Islamic societies. With the help of a small group of talented architects and scholars he established a new organisation in 1977, which would have the two-fold aim of identifying exemplars of excellence in the field of architecture, and of encouraging dialogue, debate and the exchange of ideas on the state of the built environments for Muslims. From this beginning, the Aga Khan Award for Architecture has now completed five three-year cycles of activity, and has gained authority and respect internationally as an effective organisation devoted to improving human life through the medium of architecture.

To develop the procedures and activities of the Award and to ensure organisational unity and intellectual continuity, His Highness conferred the direction of the Award upon a Steering Committee, of which he remains the Chairman. Committee meetings are organised frequently each cycle to discuss current developments, future plans and emerging directions. Complementing the work of the Steering Committee is that of the Master Jury, an independent body appointed each cycle to review the completed building projects submitted as candidates for the Award itself. Like the Steering Committees, the Master Juries bring together architects, planners and other building professionals with scholars, historians, economists and representatives of the many other fields which all contribute to the shaping of today's built environments.

Each cycle, an independent Master Jury reviews between 250 and 300 nominated projects and faces the challenge of selecting a very small number among them, which will be widely publicised throughout the world as the finest examples of architecture for Muslims today. Not only is focus placed upon each winning project but also – and perhaps more importantly – upon the collective message which, together, the projects constitute. During past cycles, as many as fifteen projects and as few as six have been selected by the successive Master Juries to share each cycle's US$500,000 prize fund. Reinforcing each group of projects, each jury has prepared a report to illustrate and define the tendencies and examples which characterise these architectural achievements.

The nine projects selected by the most recent Master Jury during the 1992 Award cycle, represent a number of new directions for architecture in our countries that will, I feel sure, continue to be developed and refined during the coming years as we enter a new century.

One of the central themes in the deliberations and written report of the 1992 Master Jury is the conviction that these nine winning projects represent solutions not limited to the Islamic world – the specific constituency of the Aga Khan Award for Architecture – but which are universal in nature. Accordingly, theJury expressed its belief that urban communities in, for example, Los Angeles or Rio de Janeiro, might benefit and learn from such efforts as those by the poorest residents of Yogyakarta, Indonesia, to improve their own environments and thereby better their own lives. Another example – and many others could be cited – is the emphasis which the jury has placed upon the appropriate use of resources and materials at hand in the creation of an harmonious and often beautiful architectural language, such as the forms and techniques developed in Syria to take advantage of the abundant availability of local stone.

Any number of the themes which concerned the 1992 Master Jury have been echoed by almost all the previous Award Juries, thereby revealing two of the most striking characteristics of the Award. The first of these is the acknowledgement that ours is not a perfect world and that, however accomplished, no single work of architecture can fully address or embody the vast array of needs and conditions, of climates and geographies, or of customs and cultures that comprise the world today. There is, however, evidence and belief in the value of dialogue and understanding, in the generous sharing of time and ideas in order to achieve the greatest benefit, and in the desire and commitment by the talented to assist their fellow-man to achieve harmony and well-being. These lofty goals will, be difficult to attain, but the composition and the working of the Jury itself reveals the extent of this commitment.

The 1992 Jury represented nine men and women who took considerable time and effort to work together as colleagues in an effort to understand and hopefully help contribute to the betterment of the built environments of that portion of the world's inhabitants who profess the faith of Islam. Like the Award organisation itself, the jury comprised the widest diversity of talents and viewpoints, drawing upon those from both the East and the West, and bringing together those from a variety of Muslim cultures with those of other faiths. Most of them shared architecture, its practice or study, as a common bond, but several came from specialised fields in other areas. It is, in fact, difficult to imagine any other platform where a group of nine such different individuals might be drawn together. There is surely no better testimony to their talents and concerns than that of the cohesion, dialogue and shared purpose which their meetings so clearly demonstrated.

This sense of unity and common purpose is the second characteristic which I referred to above and which, beyond the progress which the Award has sought to achieve in the built environment, is perhaps our greatest achievement. Many years ago Professor Mohammed Arkoun coined the phrase 'a space for freedom' to describe the Award. Not an architect, Professor Arkoun is a brilliant scholar of the history of Islamic thought, and his commitment to situating the field of architecture – and the Award – in the broader spectrum of history, including contemporary development, is but one example of the breadth and seriousness of the Award initiative. Similar examples, so different in expression and contribution, yet equally important and distinguished, are those of Oleg Grabar, for example, whose thought, effort and teaching have, in large part, shaped the conception and the study of the history of Islamic art and architecture today; Charles Correa, whose buildings and thought have transcended his native India and been commissioned, published and admired throughout the world; Ismail Serageldin, an Egyptian trained architect and planner, whose senior position as a vice-president at the World Bank attests to the scope and breadth of his concerns and expertise. Now, after fifteen years of Award activity, the list is quite long and I, myself, feel very privileged to have shared in the wisdom and commitment of all those who have been involved in the past cycles of the Award. The network of associates and correspondents who contribute to the Award in the capacity of Nominators is an exceptionally rich asset, and exemplifies the extent to which the concerns of the Award are shared by an increasingly large number of people. Of special note, too, are the members of each cycle's Technical Review programme, a unique aspect of the Award's selection process which provides the Master Jury with additional insight and expertise from the field. The series of fifteen seminars organised by the Award to date has provided unique forums for discussion world wide, bringing together local, regional and international specialists. The published proceedings of these important meetings have been distributed to students, scholars and architects worldwide.

As current secretary-general of the Award, I continuously feel indebted to the achievements of my two predecessors in that position, both of whom served as members of the 1992 Master Jury. Renata Holod led the Award from 1977 to 1980, and I have never ceased to admire the procedures, activities and the administration which she was able to create and to put into place for the organisation of the Award. All her efforts have withstood the test of time and attest to the expertise, commitment and great generosity which she demonstrated and applied. From 1981 to 1991, Saïd Zulficar reinforced and expanded the base which Holod had established and, through his personal concern, attention and commitment, established the effectiveness and prestige for which the Award is now known internationally; his compassion, concern and warmth have marked the Award forever, and both Holod and he have established a precedence which is near-impossible to follow; yet such is our task.

One other important aspect of the Award programme which merits special recognition are the archival resources at the Geneva headquarters of the Award. Since the first Award cycle, more than 1,400 building projects have been nominated for consideration, and over 1,000 of these have been fully documented in detailed monographs. The visual collections comprise more than 140,000 images, meticulously classified, key-worded and cross-referenced, and the textual collections include books, periodicals, and other publications on the architecture of the Islamic world. This unique collection, which is open for consultation for scholarly and professional purposes, has been further strengthened by the donation of two private archives from two of the pioneering architects of this century, Hassan Fathy and Michel Ecohard.

In closing, I would like to express my appreciation and to respect for the Islamic Arts Foundation in their efforts to encourage and promote better understanding and knowledge of our cultures and societies. I am happy, too, to congratulate my friend, Jalal-Uddin Ahmed, editor for the Foundation, whose continuing efforts are always admirable. It has also been a real pleasure for me, and of great benefit to the Award, to make the acquaintance of Azim Nanji, Professor of Religion at the University of Florida at Gainesville, who served as a member of the Award's 1992 Master Jury and who has edited this volume. His own efforts are but yet a further demonstration of the serious commitment which so many people around the world have made to the Award.

THE AGA KHAN PROGRAM FOR ISLAMIC ARCHITECTURE
THE VISUAL AND TEXTUAL RESOURCES

Rafique Keshavjee

A library allows a tradition to repose in safety over time. To commit a text to an archive is to insure against the fragility of human memory and to thwart the danger of loss through word of mouth. To protect a text is an act of sustained commemoration, a process vital to any tradition. As a safe repository, a library makes a discourse across time and space possible, both of which are all too often enemies of the text. But the solace offered by a security of this kind can disguise from us a price that is sometimes paid in the very act of keeping archives. To see the text as the embodiment of a tradition masks the vitality given to that tradition by human discourse and by the very process of living. This vitality exists in what one may loosely call context, which here refers to the human interaction that is vital to the development of thought within and outside the walls of academia: the recitation of great poetry, the traditions of interference from texts that are important to a community, the many and various ways of life, or the skills of building artistic expressions in a neighbourhood or a teeming city. A text is an extrication from life, while context is the meaning of a tradition in life itself. In this way a text or image can rob from context and be robbed of context. Scholarship based on library research can be seen as an attempt to revive context from text. An archive can do much service by engendering such a retrieval.

Much has been said and written about the rupture that has a place in the traditions of Muslims around the world.[1] One feature of this rupture is the absence of, or weakness in, a creative dialogue between the demands of this age and the artistic and architectural traditions of the past. For example, soon after the Aga Khan Award for Architecture was set up, the participants in the seminars associated with it came to the realisation that so little was known about the tradition, and what was known was scattered. Finally, a little of this was being transmitted. This realisation was the seed of the Aga Khan Program at Harvard and the Massachusetts Institution of Technology (MIT), part of which became a major investment in the textual and visual collection of these institutions.

Why situate the archives at Harvard and MIT? The safety of an archive over time requires confidence that such a heavy investment should survive generations from now. Among the advantages of the industrial democracies are the foundations of civil society, including stable and mature institutions. Harvard and MIT were chosen by the Aga Khan as the locus of a textual and visual archive in Islamic Art and Architecture, not just because they offered reason to anticipate long-term security but also because, as centres of excellence, they would attract faculty, professionals and students at a high academic level from around the world who could benefit from the archives.

I THE COLLECTION AT HARVARD AND MIT [2]

What is the collection today? It is enormous and rich. Both institutions together form the largest collection of Islamic art and architecture in the world. Harvard focuses on historic sources of Islamic art and architecture up to the twentieth century. Housed at the Fine Arts Library at the Fogg Museum, Harvard has a collection of last resort – what you cannot find elsewhere you will usually get here. MIT focuses on contemporary materials of the twentieth century, with English as the primary, but not only language. Areas covered at the Rotch Library, where the collection is located, are the architecture and urbanism of Muslim countries and communities. Included are works on urban history, regional and urban planning, books by or about architects, architectural and planning education, architectural preservation and conservation, urban and housing finance and administration. Although English is the primary language collected, works in Arabic, Persian, Urdu and Turkish are also collected.

What are the strengths and weakness of such a collection? This question is hard to answer as it is such a large and diverse collection.

a) Harvard
The Textual Collection

Given Harvard's history, it is no surprise that by the time the Aga Khan Program came into being the collection was already substantial and of some historical interest, including the only image showing the famous view of Tangiers which Matisse enjoyed from his hotel room.

Serious collecting in this area had begun after World War I and by the time the Program started, the total Islamic collection at Harvard, scattered throughout the many libraries, was well in excess of 100,000 titles, of which a sizable segment was devoted to Islamic Art. Over the first decade of the Program about 5,000 titles were acquired. More significantly, it has a professional staff dedicated exclusively to the field. It can therefore cast a finer net in its acquisitions, and obtain items like exhibition or auction catalogues which may prove vital in tracing important works of art.

The weaknesses? It has no sixteenth-century or earlier titles, which would naturally be better represented in older European counterparts such as the British Library or the Bibliothèque Nationale. The librarians decided that the huge cost of acquiring these could be better spent on a larger number of newer titles with a wider range. The collection is not particularly strong in languages such as Malay, Indonesian or Bengali, but the library has an arrangement with a central resource shared by a number of universities, from which books can be obtained within a week. The librarians thought it may help those contemplating using the collection to also be aware of what the collection is *not*: for example, it does not collect manuscripts; nor does it house the collection of Prince Sadruddin Aga Khan. Finally, it is not equipped to serve as a picture resource for general purposes – a commercial company like the Bettman Archive is far better equipped.

The Visual Collection

The collection is based mainly at the Fine Arts Library situated at the Fogg Museum. By the 1920s there were 20,000 visual records, including nineteenth- and early twentieth-century photographs. The images were mainly of the Middle East, including Cairo, Istanbul, various parts of Syria, Palestine and Iraq. When Professor Oleg Grabar joined the faculty, the visual collection grew more rapidly until it was over 60,000 in 1979. Since the Aga Khan Program started in 1980, the collection grew in leaps. More importantly, the diversity of the Muslim world was taken more into consideration: Iran, the Maghrib, Indo-Pakistan and South-East Asia began to strengthen the collection as well. It now stands at 135,000 images of the Islamic artistic and architectural heritage.

b) MIT

MIT's collection, which focuses more on the contemporary built environment, is much newer, and thus understandably smaller, amounting to about 6,000 titles. Each year about 400 titles are added through purchases and donations. For ease of reference a large number of images have been put on a videodisc called *Images of Islamic Architecture*. The visual collection is neither comprehensive nor all-revealing. Images are always collected with a particular purpose in mind, such as a research project or site visit, so what they reveal will reflect the intention of the researcher. Moreover, the quality of the images will vary, as many of those who took the images were students of architecture rather than of photography.

II THE OUTREACH PROGRAM

A few years ago the Aga Khan Program established a collaborative relationship with two academic institutions in the Muslim world to provide an element of outreach for the enormous investment at Harvard and MIT. One is with Amman University in Jordan and the other with Dawood College in Karachi, Pakistan. This programme has already been discussed elsewhere. The libraries, for their part, have undertaken their share, focusing primarily on identifying the parameters of a core collection on Islamic art and architecture. This task covers more than just the rather knotty issue of how to categorise the visual resources, including the identification of the major monuments of Islamic architecture, as well as indicating the enormously diverse range of architecture to be found in many cultures in which Muslims live, when a student would only think of Islamic as Middle Eastern. This project tries to answer the following questions: what should a core collection of reference books and important scholarly works look like? What is the most important image of the tradition of Islamic architecture for use in an introductory course? How can one categorise it to provide ease of access? Where can one purchase texts in this field?

It would not be surprising if a university in the Muslim world sought more than advice and information, and hoped for an actual part of the massive collection of the Aga Khan Program. Unfortunately, the costs of replicating such a collection are vast, and a large number of images, particularly at Harvard were obtained under copyright, so to produce each one would require the arduous labour of an approval, plus the likelihood of a fee.

Nevertheless, the entire collection of the Aga Khan Program at Harvard and MIT is available to the academic community of both institutions, as well as to visiting scholars of other universities and academic institutions. Moreover, the visual archives at MIT have to their credit an unusual collection of over 100,00 images illustrating a broad spectrum of Islamic architecture, both historical and contemporary. Predominantly in 35mm slide format and copyright-free, holdings of the archive also include black and white photographic prints and negatives, plans and drawings. Each year the library acquires about 3,000 more images directly from architects, professional photographers, travellers and students.

NOTES

1 Mohamed Arkoun is particularly trenchant on this. See, for example, his contributions in the publications of the Aga Khan Award for Architecture.

2 My gratitude to Andras Riedlemeyer, Jeff Spurr and Merrill Smith for information on the collections, and to the librarians who prepared the material from which I have liberally quoted.

AKAA, 1983, Hajj Terminal, Jeddah, Saudi Arabia

INTENTIONS AND CHALLENGES

Nader Ardalan

The fact that the Aga Khan Award for Architecture is now accepted worldwide as the premier prize in the field of Islamic architecture, stands as a justification of His Highness the Aga Khan's vision and his organisational commitment. The Award speaks for the urgent need for a greater awareness of the architectural heritage of the diverse Muslim cultures and the search for excellence in the newly built environments of those lands. It is with delight and pride that I write about the Award.

As well tuned instruments of the aesthetic, social and technical high ground of human creation, the Awards and their related programmes can play even more significant roles in the future development of Islamic cultures, and contribute not only to specifically Muslim thought, but also to the human condition and the innovative processes of human adaptations to a dramatically changing world.

It is with these aims in mind that the following brief comments have been set forth. They are organised in four sections, which relate to the *context* within which the Aga Khan Awards were first conceived; interpretations of the *intentions* that motivated the formulation of the Awards process; an assemblage of the *judgements* to date on the relative success and shortcomings of the process; and a conclusion with a personal recommendation on some of the *future challenges* that the Awards process may consider in the next cycle of its growth.

The Context

The Aga Khan Awards began in the mid 1970s, in the aftermath of the energy crisis of 1973, the last Arab-Israeli conflict, and the surge of petro-dollars for the OPEC countries. It also began with the vision of a great man seeking further self-realisation as the spiritual and material leader of an important Muslim community.

In the history of the philosophy of aesthetics and architecture, however, the Awards process occurred precisely at the threshold of the contemporary world's freedom of bondage from the Bauhaus and the ahistorical mind-set that had held sway since the end of World War II. Such seminal works as Robert Venturi's *Complexity and Contradiction in Architecture,* were the first manifestations of this new cycle of thought. The release of this stranglehold also partially freed the Muslim world from its homage to Western architectural thought.

Interestingly enough, however, since it has taken at least one or two decades for the popular world views to filter into the mainstream of the Third World and to have an impact on its actions, most of the Muslim world remained in a state of architectonic limbo, characterised by a few trends. The most compelling trend in the large cities of Muslim countries was to continue without too much sophistication about new or old world styles, and to slowly slide into a characterless, polluted urban 'pastiche of modernity', consumed by the monopolising pressures of industry and mass communication. In the hinterlands of small towns and villages, where the vast majority of the population lived, the trend was for more of the same – a watered-down version of traditional, vernacular architecture using limited, local resources.

Finally, sprinkled as rare gems throughout the Muslim lands, there also existed the surviving remnants of the cultural monuments of the different Islamic nations and the private architectural treasures of those means.

As a case in point, in the 1960s and 70s, the newly educated professional élites of the Middle East naturally perpetuated the modernist lessons gained in their educational periods of the 1950s and 60s, spent either in the West or in Western-based colleges in the Middle East. The leaders of the Islamic countries encouraged this trend, for it brought a visual image of modernity to their nations.

Few, very few, professionals in the Muslim world understood or wanted to accept the Western world shift of architectural thinking. They were too busy convincing the decision makers, and their clients, of the 'modern gospel according to Mies van der Rohe', or Le Corbusier, which they had recently gained after much investment of time, money and personal effort. Some were convinced that the West had lost its way and did not realise the mistake it was making by giving up the Modern movement.

A small faction appreciated that the 'moment was right' to rediscover and enhance the great traditions of their respective building histories. Hassan Fathy, the distinguished Egyptian architect, was one such visionary. Fewer still saw the moment as ripe for a 'new creation' – an innovative leap that integrated traditional and contemporary opportunities.

Within this context the Aga Khan Award for Architecture was born.

FROM ABOVE: Hajj Terminal, Jeddah, Saudi Arabia; AKAA, 1980, interior of the auditorium at the Inter-Continental Hotel, Mecca, Saudi Arabia; AKAA, 1986, Saudi Ministry of Foreign Affairs, Riyadh, Saudi Arabia

Intentions

The Aga Khan Award for Architecture is intended to encourage an understanding and awareness of the strength and diversity of Muslim cultural traditions which, when combined with an enlightened use of modern technology for contemporary society, will result in buildings more appropriate for the Islamic world of tomorrow.

His Highness the Aga Khan, 1976.

The Aga Khan was one of the few men of adequate vision and personal capability at this time to seize the historic moment and to begin the search for relevant answers. A very small circle of trusted individuals (mostly non-architects) from the Aga Khan's own staff was organised, initially to search for answers from informed and inter-ested persons around the world. A handful of selected people were then asked to help design and elaborate the parameters and governance of what became The Aga Khan Award for Architecture. It was a distinct honour to have been selected as one of the first three persons, who then in turn became the founding members of the Steering Committee of the Awards Program. Intentions have always been the most valued of considerations among Muslims of all walks of life. What you intend to do is valued almost as much as what you actually do.

Fortunately, the Aga Khan has revealed many of his intentions and those of the Steering Committee of the Awards, through numerous published speeches, seminar proceedings and other publications. An extensive and graphically impressive publication programme has docu-mented the evolution and growth of the Awards process. *Mimar* magazine, since its founding under the capable editorship of Hassan-Uddin Khan, and until its recent closure, was one of these notable periodicals devoted to architecture in the developing world, and Islamic culture in particular.

As would be expected, the words of the Aga Khan have tended to be more conceptual than prescriptive. In fact, a policy has been established for the Awards programmes to avoid specific design directions or proscriptive codes. To quote the Aga Khan:

It would be tempting . . . to propagate a particular type of design solution, but this we have absolutely rejected. Similarly, it is not our intention . . . to found a particular school of architectural thought . . .

This policy, while noble and befitting at the onset of the Awards process, should perhaps be reviewed and re-evaluated after the results and experience gained in five Award cycles.

Other intentions have been demonstrated by the selection of persons entrusted to implement the Aga Khan's intentions. The 'companions of the search' have varied over time and their influence on the ultimate path followed has depended upon the relative longevity of their proximity to the source of the Awards. The original founding members of the Steering Committee of the Awards had a strong impact on the formation of the Award process. Over time, the 'companions' have grown to include many more members than the Award Steering Committees, including the various distinguished members of Master Juries, the office of the Secretary General of the Awards, and the Aga Khan Trust for Culture. This diverse, international group of individuals has represented a broad, concrete spectrum of people equipped to handle the relevant aspects of the principle question: 'How can the Awards premiate and raise greater consciousness regarding an accommodating Islamic environment?' A yet unaccomplished analysis of the 'excluded advisors' might also yield an interesting insight into the intentions of the Award. Still other manifestations of the intentions have been the institutions and organisations established over time and in different geographic locations to carry out different aspects of the intention. These organisational responses, on the whole, have tended to reflect the larger institutional structures of which they have been a part.

As a case in point, after the establishment of the Awards Organisation, first in Philadelphia and its subsequent, now permanent, home in Geneva, the Aga Khan Programs in Islamic Architecture at Harvard University and MIT in Cambridge, Massachusetts were launched. These programmes reflect some of the original Award visions, but the MIT Program under Professor William Porter and, until recently, Professor Ronald Lewcock, has tended to emphasise regional vernacularisation with less emphasis on technological innovation. This characteristic is particularly interesting, given that MIT is a leading high-tech institution of learning.

The Harvard University Programs, on the other hand, have focused on two different domains. At the Fogg Art Museum, originally under Professor Oleg Grabar and now under the direction of Professor Gulru Necipoglu, the emphasis has been on the history of Islamic art and architecture. At the Graduate School of Design, Professor Francois Vigier and Mona Serageldin have focused on Third World urban development projects and city management. Aga Khan Architectural Programs have also been instituted at the College of Fine Arts in Lahore, Pakistan and Jordan University in Amman.

The more newly formed Aga Khan Trust for Culture under the direction of Professor John de Monchaux, including the Historic Cities Preservation Program, has also been established recently.

The Judgements

By far, however, the most immediately measurable deeds have been the actual Awards presented to selected built architectural projects. There have now been five Award cycles, commencing in 1980 and recurring every three years. The patterns of the Awards have been commented upon periodically by members of the Aga Khan pro-

grammes, the professional and popular press, and by the informal reflections of concerned architects around the world. Over time, my own personal impressions of the awarded projects are that they represent a significant achievement of consciousness which have generally fallen into four categories as described below:

1 Preservation and adaptive reuse
2 Contemporary use of traditional vocabularies
3 Community development for the masses
4 Relevant innovations

Recognition of conservation and reuse projects is an accepted formula for appropriate action on identity presentation by cultures of all lands and faiths. The older the historical roots of that community, the larger the choice of palette, and the more numerous the examples. While this field should be a recognised area of focus, it does not bring a new vision, nor does it foster a field that would otherwise be neglected. In short, UNESCO and other cultural conservation institutions, as well as the respective countries themselves, have and will promote this subject independently of the Awards process.

Closely allied, however, with the previous category is the architectural design approach concerning the contemporary reuse of traditional building vocabularies. This category neatly grows out of the former, because in many instances the preservation process produces the craftsmen that are able to construct the traditional patterns and techniques in new buildings.

The Awards process has recognised these two allied categories in all five cycles. In many ways, because of the heartfelt, sometimes romantic attachment of most people to their traditions, the Awards legitimised this nostalgic tendency, which until the 1970s was philosophically untenable in the modern architectural movements of the 1940s, 50s and 60s. As a consequence, however, the Awards have sometimes become characterised, or even criticised, as being mainly a vernacular, historically backward-looking endeavour.

The architecture of the poor, or more socially related participatory development programmes has also found its 'niche' in the Awards process. While not always exhibiting architectural environments of great aesthetic quality, the selected projects show profound social commitment. However, a silently voiced reservation has always been associated with these projects concerning their architectural merits and the 'ghettoisation' of their inhabitants.

Of the fifty-seven awarded projects to date, ninety-two per cent have been relegated to the first three categories, and only eight per cent, thus far, to the category of relevant innovations. The five selected projects in the latter category have been the Hajj Air Terminal and the Intercontinental Hotel and Foreign Ministry Building in Saudi Arabia; the Sherefudin Mosque in Bosnia; and the Parliament Building in Bangladesh.

This tendency has been commented upon in every

Chairman's Award, 1980, Riad House, Sakkara Rd, Egypt, Hassan Fathy

AKAA, 1980, Inter-Continental Hotel, Mecca, Saudi Arabia

cycle of the Award process from its inception, and has even resulted in a number of dissenting, minority jury statements. What are the reasons behind this pattern? Some salient, possible explanations raised to date in the Award publications and the press have been as follows:

1   An anti-modern bias of the Awards.
2   A bias against Western architects working in Islamic countries, who may be the main proponents of technologically innovative projects.
3   A possible shortage of truly outstanding projects representing innovative integrations.
4   A lack of agreement by the Award Steering Committees, Juries, and Technical Committees as to what constitutes architectural excellence in these 'new creations'.

It may be that all of the above are to various degrees true. It may be that the 'questions' are more easily asked than 'answered'. It may also be that a fundamental premise of the formula developed by the Awards process and programmes needs to be re-evaluated after fifteen years of testing, removing an obstacle that could free new dimensions of heightened creativity and allow it to pour forth.

For many years there has been an Award 'taboo' regarding the development of a particular school of architectural theory. This hands-off policy may have had some merit at the initial stages, but by default or intention, the programmes have become identified with the projects chosen. These projects, as has been demonstrated, have been overwhelmingly characterised by regional vernacularism and historicism. Therefore, the Award stands at its own critical threshold today. Will it champion a high standard of architecture that nourishes and accommodates an Islamic way of life in the twenty-first century? Or will it be the captive, conservative voice of a way whose architectural expressions are frozen and repertoire is well known? Will new societal forms and technical functions remain without an 'Islamic touch' for lack of attention, and will the search for new directions be stifled?

For many years, I have personally observed in both the Awards process and the various related academic and architectural programmes a constraint that has been placed upon the systematic intellectual research for new directions related to both old and new programmatic building functions.

In retrospect, while a pluralism of ideas and design attitudes is a necessary and healthy attribute, there is always a danger of having lost the 'moment' and of having too much of a 'laissez-faire' attitude. Imagine how far we could have come today if coincident with the espousing of regional vernacularism and historical preservation, the Aga Khan programmes had also nurtured and supported, with the same level of cultural sensitivity, more research and development of new theories of innovative architectural and engineering designs related to the principle ecological and cultural zones of the Muslim world?

Future Challenges

How are new theories of innovative design generated and upon what principles? 'Necessity is the mother of all invention', it has been said. The new architectural paradigms should answer the needs of the whole person, their respective community needs, and show an awareness of the global issues confronting humankind at the dawning of the twenty-first century.

'A person is at once body, soul and spirit – having physical needs, an affective life of the soul and an intelligence which surpasses both these planes', Titus Burchkardt, the noted Swiss philosopher of Islamic art, once observed. Within the Islamic communities, the elements of the built environments should meet their respective regional physical requirements, delight the communal soul of their citizenry and allow a spiritual dimension to shine through. Globally, clear evidence exists that there are physical requirements that need to be understood and not exceeded, if not fully accommodated.

We are also learning that what actually initiates and then accompanies the physical adaptations to this surface belt of the 'Gaia', are the global souls' quest for new strategies of survival, manifested through climatic, biological, geological and hydrological changes. Through this process, we are just beginning to intuit and sense the pure wonder and ordered dynamism of the cosmic spirit as it unfolds into yet more new patterns.

The new architectural paradigm of our communities should respond locally to these global requirements and realisations, which have never before confronted human kind in such sheer numbers and magnitude. Such challenges as the population explosion, urban pollution, global warming, desertification, ozone depletion, and biodiversity depletion, to name but a few, have largely not been faced since the last Ice Age.

With over a billion persons spanning the globe from the Atlantic to the Pacific Oceans, the Islamic cultures of the world encompass all of the bio-climatic zones of the earth, within which exist the population concentrations of humanity. Regional design answers to global needs by their respective Muslim cultures can carry a component of culture-specific responses and a significant degree of universal concerns.

These responses can be characterised by the perpetuation of design attitudes that are retrospective or progressively timeless in their root inspirations. The Aga Khan programmes can nurture and lead the way through the established network of Awards, academia and cultural institutions. To date, however, it has tended to primarily recognise small-scale, regional, historically retrospective directions. Few innovative directions have been found, consciously researched or developed by the Award.

With the world population explosion occurring in many of the poorer Islamic countries, the Awards programmes could simply follow the path of 'more of the same'. The

Kampung Improvement Programmes of Indonesia, or the East Wahdat Upgrading Programmes of Jordan, and other 'sites and services' programmes of the World Bank, stand as undeniable highlights of significant social and, at times, ecological programmes that should be encouraged. They generally fail, however, to achieve the same degree of environmental qualitative merit which was also the original goal of the Award. It is time that other institutions of the Aga Khan Program took on the social programmes and gave them the attention they deserve, so freeing the Awards Program to attend to the equally important issues that have been left wanting.

In a somewhat associated and similar manner, can we reconsider the focus of the Awards on the vernacular, to the near exclusion of technological innovation? The vernacular regionalism of Hassan Fathy of Egypt, and his distinguished 'students', such as Abdel-Wahed El Wakil and Abdelhalem Ibrahim Abdelhalim, are acknowledged examples of the reuse of a historically known vocabulary that has been resuscitated by their fine efforts. Similarly, when implemented with sensitivity – as Turgut Cansever has accomplished in Turkey – this approach has found its just place in the project types chosen by the Awards.

However, rarely has a successful vernacular approach been effectively applied to a large, social development project. The village of New Gourna, Egypt, by Hassan Fathy may be an isolated example, but there is some question as to its overall social success.

Undoubtedly, the greatest pitfall that these social improvement programmes, and the historical preservation and élite vernacular regionalism approaches bring to mind, is that the Awards Program has become captive to them. The Aga Khan Award's search for 'new creations' in architecture and community development has been stripped of its concern for the 'enlightened use of modern technology for contemporary society' – which was one of the pivotal intentions of His Highness the Aga Khan at the inception of the Awards. In fact, the 1992 cycle of Awards omitted any recognition of advanced technology and did not award any contemporary utilitarian public concerns such as hospitals, shopping centres, office buildings, transportation centres and so on.

The editor of the *Encyclopedia Britannica*, Harry Ashmore, noted that his

> nomination for the most compelling statistic compiled so far in this extravagantly charted age, is the finding that ninety per cent of all scientists and engineers who ever lived are still alive and practising. At a minimum, this means that most of the goods and services that sustain and shape our civilisation have been conceived or perfected by the contemporary generation.

If inventions and the cutting edge of scientific innovation in architectural design and technology are not proportionately generated and poetically attuned in Muslim lands, they will most likely be deferred to other cultures to discover and perfect. For Muslim cultures, they will then become items of import and not *sui generis* to themselves. The Muslim societies' vitality and the sense of pride associated with intellectual advancement could erode further, leaving an intellectual and economic imperialism from more advanced societies to continue battling with the traditional values in most Muslim lands.

These bleak cataclysmic projections may never occur, since the sheer complexity of human societies generate a kaleidoscope of varying adaptations. Yet, the signs of such dark futures evident in the 1970s when the Awards Program began, are still evident today, and could multiply if they are not counteracted.

So what effect has the Awards Program had on the trends and the built environments of Islamic lands?

From a long-term view, the last fifteen years could be perceived as the first stage of a long 'Great Work' of transformation. Since the Award's quest for perfection is, by definition, both of a spiritual and material nature, it could be said to resemble an alchemical process of three stages. First, there is the purification stage, which is achieved only by means of repeated distillation and solidification. The first five cycles of the Awards may therefore have simply distilled out the irrelevant matter – at times called 'ridding the subject of its attle'. It is possible, therefore, to accept that the awarded projects to date, as a whole, reflect a genuine concern to sustain Muslim modes, which have yet to discover a 'pure ore'.

The second degree of perfection is attained when the same subject has been cooked, digested and fixed into an incombustible substance. This stage has yet to occur. With critical reappraisal, insight and rededication it could commence as soon as a greater degree of purification, moving towards an ultimate state of conceptual truth, is reached. This stage requires the shedding of the 'husks' of known images and the seeking of the hidden 'incombustible', archetypal and environmentally sustainable forms.

The third and final stage appears when the subject has been fermented, multiplied and brought to ultimate perfection. At this state, spirit and matter reach perfect union in the 'philosopher's stone', and masterpieces of architectural and the human environment are attained, emanating the pure light of divine presences.

'Our method is a method of alchemy. It is a question of drawing out the subtle organism of light, for over it is the mountain under which man is prisoner.'

THE AGA KHAN AWARD FOR ARCHITECTURE

A Critical Commentary

WAYNE ATTOE

Conceived in 1976, and established in 1977, the Aga Khan Award has now seen five cycles of awards at three-year intervals, enough to warrant examination as a force in contemporary architecture.[1] Based on its fifteen-year history, what are the characteristics of the Aga Khan Award for Architecture? For one thing it is more complex than other award programmes due to its broad geographical and cultural scope and its programmatic range. It represents the geographical extent of Islam, 'from Mali to Malaysia, the problems of rural and urban populations, and of widely varying incomes in very different environments' (1983[2]). It does not honour individual architects as the Pritzker Prize does; nor new construction or designs on paper, like many other award programmes. Rather, it recognises architecture that has been in use.[3]

The values of pluralism, tolerance, and understanding guide the process: 'At no time has the Award tried to endorse a particular "style", nor has it taken a position on an ideological plane that would exclude any dimension of this multi-faceted search'. It has sought to create a 'space of freedom where intellectual debate among those concerned with the built environment of Muslims could proceed unhindered and uninhibited . . . ' (1986)

As there is no over-riding or absolute standard against which winners are measured, judgements by each Master Jury are conditioned by the make-up of that jury and by world circumstances. In fact, due to this absence of clearly articulated standards, and the range of work submitted, in its early years the Award recognised effort as much as achievement in the building project. In 1986 the Jury explained that the lack of balance in that cycle's award was not due to bias on its part, but what it had to respond to. That same jury was 'keenly aware that its choice would be interpreted as "sending a message" of a direction or directions which architects in Islamic societies ought to or might follow. Few of the nominated projects could perform this role'. In other words, these were the best of this group, but not necessarily worthy of emulation.

Similarly, most of the awards in 1983 represented 'not the ultimate in architectural excellence, but steps in a process of discovery, still an incomplete voyage towards many promising frontiers'. The absence of clear standards means that the judges themselves must create the norms

for the role of Islamic architecture in people's lives, and a result is an intriguing process of qualification in which jury reports are dotted with cautions and conditions. The 1989 report cautioned that 'these decisions should not be seen as an endorsement of all the implications of the project involved, nor do they imply the rejection of values expressed in projects which were not premiated'. Such qualifying remarks indicate a sense of a standard to which projects might aspire, but do not offer clues to what the standard is. (This is not unusual in judgemental criticism.)

Of course there are criteria. In establishing the Award, His Highness the Aga Khan specified an intent 'to encourage an architecture in the spirit of Islam, an architecture that would enrich the future physical environment of the Muslim world [and] recognise completed projects which meet today's needs while in close harmony with their own culture and climate'. A 'framework of concerns' was developed, too, including 'sensitivity to the ecological and cultural context and to social needs'; creative use of local initiative and resources; and potential to stimulate related development elsewhere in the Islamic world (Introduction, 1980). These goals and concerns do not offer strict norms against which designs can be judged, but factors that are open to interpretation. It was admitted from the start that 'there would be a variety of definitions of architecture, and in particular, of architecture in Islamic society today' (Introduction, 1980). Hence there is a 'softness' in standards which allows latitude for unexpected factors. In fact it is remarkable that an award process established by such a powerful individual could still be so lacking in apparent control. I have trouble imagining a process which is more professionally responsible, yet not élitist.

Noteworthy about these criteria set by the Aga Khan is their social bias. Most other well known awards in architecture are for 'excellence' or for consistent, good, professional performance by an individual. To recognise buildings for their social utility, as this Award does as well as for aesthetic or technical accomplishments, is unusual among major architecture awards, yet it is reasonable. Why not honour a complex that has positive effects on people's lives? But this quality is not easy to measure, and jurors, in making their judgements, must rely on the reports of technical teams that visit finalist projects.

Do jurors ever agree that a design is good enough? Yes, but it is noteworthy that juror agreement is not necessarily about the all-important social considerations, but about achievements that are technological or in a modernist aesthetic – what I would call an 'international standard' of quality. For example, almost all the jurors in 1983 felt that the Hajj Terminal in Jeddah was 'in a class by itself, its structure a magnificent achievement of twentieth-century technology' (1983). Such an agreement about the value of technology and modernist aesthetics undoubtedly reflects the international Muslim plus non-Muslim composition of the juries. And it is probably appropriate that this 'international standard' of excellence outside the specific Muslim social realm is part of the award process, for without it the Award might seem too narrow and parochial.

The softness of the standards and the impact of individual personalities in the course of jury deliberations produces a remarkable behaviour that adds credibility to the Award process. Juries communicate with one another over the spans of three or more years. One jury referred to a previous report and in doing so 'indicated a continued emphasis on the search for relevant forms and designs to anticipate and satisfy future needs', in short, concurrence with an earlier value that gives added weight to that value. In 1986 the jury recommended reconsideration of a finalist in the next Award cycle, because the nominee had not yet been used enough to be tested socially and functionally; in effect saying, 'we couldn't make the Award, but probably you should'. Similarly, the 1989 Jury recommended reconsideration of projects it found necessary to pass over because they needed more time to be properly appraised. That aspect of the process carry-over from one jury to the next links individual juries as a kind of Super Jury, one less limited by the exigencies of a moment in time. This does not happen often, but it is a marvellous corrective tool that can offer a modicum of direction in the absence of a stricter set of standards. Particularly notable in this regard was the decision of one jury not to honour Louis I Kahn's National Assembly Building in Dhaka, followed by a subsequent jury's decision to convey the honour.

Disagreements between jury members are sometimes openly discussed and in fact become indicators of contemporary controversies in the profession at large. In 1983 some jury members felt strongly that in spite of its elegance and beauty, the mud mosque in Niono, Mali, by a master mason, 'was not in a class with the architecture of more sophisticated societies, that it represents the last efforts of a traditional culture that cannot survive long; other jurors saw it in its continuity and poetry as representing a major source of continuing inspiration' (1983). The controversy over Kahn's complex in Dhaka had at its heart the feeling that there was a bias at the time against modernist design in the Awards Program. At another time a juror pointed out that in making awards on the basis of a majority vote, the Award's mandate for pluralism is

denied, since minority opinion (and taste) is over-ruled. Through a published minority opinion, however, this problem can be compensated for, and has been – as the Kahn controversy indicates. It is noteworthy that some juries choose to make the awards unanimous following their debate, and others do not.

In the absence of concrete standards from the Award Program itself, individual juries establish their own criteria, or frame the more general ones in ways that seem more specific. Whether these criteria are bought to the process by the jurors, or emerge in the course of jurors' discussions of nominated projects, they provide *ad hoc* standards and, perhaps as important, a mechanism for explaining choices to a professional world that takes great interest in the Aga Khan Program. For example, the first Master Jury constructed 'a framework of concerns, identifying seven different directions towards an architecture more appropiate for the Islamic world of tomorrow:

1   The social premises for future architectural development
2   The search for consistency with historical context
3   The search for preservation of traditional heritage
4   Restoration
5   The search for contemporary use of traditional language
6   The search for innovation
7   The search for appropriate building systems'.

By contrast, the 1992 jury chose projects 'whose essence, directness and modesty have lessons for the world at large', and categorised them in terms of enchancing urban environments and generating new architectural languages. The standards are quite different, yet that is not a problem; their role is to aid each jury in establishing its own basis for a consistent evaluation in that cycle within the general intentions of the overall Award Program.

The most frequent group of winners have been the ones who have concentrated upon rehabilitation/conservation projects of communities and individual structures. This might be because it is easier to achieve replication than it is to achieve a new or higher standard in a new effort; or because existing construction is readily identified with Muslim life; or because for whatever reasons, it appears that contemporary construction in much of the Islamic world seldom has been successful in achieving the other goals set out by the awards, namely those linking past and present. For example, notably few awards have gone to industrial and commercial buildings and complexes. But it is asserted by one observer, at least, that over the period of the five award cycles, the quality of contemporary designs nominated has improved, so we could well see a reduction in the percentage of conservation schemes and more new designs in future cycles.

The high purpose of the Award, and the seriousness of jury members, inclines some juries to influence and even direct future design through recommendations to practising designers and their clients. In this way the Award might be seen to directly influence Islamic architecture in the future as well as recognise past achievements. The 1980 jury was deeply conscious of the need for future evolution of Islamic architecture to meet the urgent needs of their impatient masses. Search for appropriate forms of low-cost housing is one such area of urgent crisis in many Muslim societies. A good deal of intensive research and analysis is needed to identify cost-effective, indigenous and innovative solutions to the architectural forms which are most suitable for economic, cultural and technological needs of the Muslim world (1980).

In 1986 there was something akin to a lecture on the value of cultural continuity:

When a nation loses its sense of identity, and therefore its pride in itself, it is deprived of creative genius . . . Two dangers threathen continuity. On the one hand, there are possibilities of distortion though the process of reinterpretation and re-evaluation of cultures in the face of new challenges and opportunities, and of undue external influences . . . On the other hand, there is the extreme severity and urgency of the urban expansion of the Third World . . . Housing may now be the most important of the problems that architects in Islamic societies have to face . . . There is also the ecological responsibility that the architect has to assume towards the countryside (1986).

The jury indicated that 'social housing, and public and building types exhibiting modern architectural expression are especially relevant categories to be encouraged in the Islamic world'. Through such lecturing and advice, and the recognition of particular building projects, the Award itself seems capable of altering conditions through the increased attention it brings to Islamic architecture and particular issues in building for Muslim communities. The Award is undoubtedly shaping design while judging it. At the same time, some juries are uncomfortable with their potential influence: 'The Award Jury was aware of the danger of bringing to its task a uniformity of approach and taste' (1986). Each Award cycle is in some ways a barometer or an indicator of pressing issues felt by each jury: social conscience; technological innovation; reconciliation of tradition and contemporary; popular culture versus high design; developed cultures versus developing ones, and so on. In 1986,

few projects excited any passions. The difficulties in agreeing on more than a small number of works of quality may also reflect the issues of doubt and reassessment mentioned above, and are an indication of a crisis in creativity and innovation (1986).

The history of such a crisis and of the changing and constant ideals in Islamic architecture are being capsulised in the series of Aga Khan Awards.

My characterisation of the Award as soft in its standards, conditional and fluid is not critical, but descriptive. Repeatedly it is metaphors of discovery that jurors use to characterise their process and the very designs they are evaluating. There are no certain answers for architecture in an Islamic world, at least not now. Instead, jurors say, there is a search, a voyage, and there are these

milestones on the paths of improvement in conception and practice towards a more enabling and human environment that allows contemporary Muslim societies to solve their problems and to express themselves in works of beauty and value.

This sense of a journey in order to discover the answers, rather than to impose them; to make detours and then course corrections, is what keeps the Aga Khan Awards process vital.

NOTES

1 Membership of the Award jury changes each cycle, and nominations for the Award are limited to built projects which have been in use at least two years. (Nominations come from a network of individuals chosen for this role.) Each jury selects a group of finalists from the lists of nominees which typically number over two hundred. A technical team visits the selected group and compiles a report which the jury then uses to choose a smaller set of winning projects. The number of award-winners has ranged from six to fifteen in a given cycle; additional 'honourable mentions' were awarded once as well.

2 Year references are from the officially published reports of jury decisions for those cycles.

3 There have been two exceptions when Hassan Fathy in 1980, and Rifat Chadirji in 1986, received 'Chairman's Awards' for their career contributions to architecture.

PAGE 104: AKAA, 1989, National Assembly Building, Dhaka, Bangladesh; OVERLEAF LEFT, FROM ABOVE: National Assembly Building, Dhaka, Bangladesh; AKAA, 1983, the Great Mosque of Niono, Niono, Mali; OVERLEAF RIGHT, FROM ABOVE: AKAA, 1980, Water Towers, Kuwait City, Kuwait; AKAA, 1983, Hajj Terminal, Jeddah, Saudi Arabia

FROM ABOVE, L to R: AKAA, 1986, Social Security Complex, Istanbul, Turkey; AKAA, 1986, Honourable Mention, Historic Sites Development, Istanbul, Turkey; AKAA, 1980, Turkish Historical Society, Ankara, Turkey; AKAA, 1992, Demir Holiday Village, Bodrum, Turkey

AGA KHAN ARCHITECTURAL AWARDS AND TURKISH ARCHITECTURE

Dogan Tekeli

Axilla Ilhan, the prominent Turkish poet and writer, believes that the main reason for the primacy of Western culture and civilisation today is its ability to renew itself without imitating other cultures. If one accepts this thesis, one might say that certain societies have remained less developed because they have been unable to renew themselves.

More particularly, notwithstanding their rich cultural and architectural heritage, a majority of Muslim societies today find themselves living in a deteriorating built environment. Can these poor conditions be improved in such a way as to enable these societies to attain a contemporary built environment, one of the most important factors in creating a healthy and productive tomorrow? How can one stimulate concern and create a common social consensus on the issues that face these societies?

I believe that the Aga Khan Award for Architecture, established in 1977 by his Highness the Aga Khan, has constituted a means of forming a social consensus and building awareness about the quality of the built environment. Established with the aim of discovering, identifying and putting forward extraordinary architectural achievements in the Muslim world, the Award evoked enthusiasm and hope in Turkey as well as in other countries. I have had the opportunity of observing the activities of the Award closely since its establishment. In particular, it should, from the seminars organised by the Award and the publications resulting from the seminars, have helped to broaden the intellectual perspectives of most of us who practise architecture in Muslim countries.

In Turkey, the appreciation and interest in architectural work, the activities of the Award and the messages conveyed by the consecutive juries have also resulted in a degree of controversy, disapproval and strong criticism.

In particular there was a strong response to some of the projects which received awards during the second and fourth cycles in 1983 and 1989 respectively. Many critical articles appeared in architectural magazines from architects, educators and critics.

In both cycles two small resort houses received awards from among thirty or so nominations from Turkey. The respective master juries, which included individuals of international fame, did not consider the large-scale buildings valued and chosen by the Turkish nominators worthy of the Award. On the other hand, during the first four cycles, nominees outside Turkey such as the Hajj Terminal in Jeddah, the Ministry of Foreign Affairs Building in Riyadh, and the National Assembly Building in Dhaka, were recognised. These were large-scale architectural works by major foreign architectural firms. Turkish architectural circles perceived these results as conveying a message from the international juries that implied that local architects could only master small-scale buildings, restoration work or the application of primitive technology. Large-scale architectural works of quality, however, could only be produced by foreign architectural firms. There was a strong note of disapproval at the implications of such a message.

After the Awards of the fifth cycle in in 1992, which did not include any large-scale works, Peter Davey of *The Architectural Review* noted: 'The Jury's concern to find new buildings of directness and modesty which have lessons for the world at large has possibly precluded the inclusion of large commercial and bureaucratic buildings that enhance ordinary life. Perhaps they do not exist in the Islamic world: perhaps they are only made in the West by exceptional clients and architects'.

One way of balancing the perspectives which result from such a perceived problem is to keep in mind that architectural excellence can only be achieved under certain circumstances. It relates to the intention of the client, the skill, knowledge and experience of the architect, the knowledge, and experience of the construction workers and the attitude of the users towards the building. In Third World countries in general, it is easier for these circumstances to come together in the case of small-scale buildings. On the other hand, in the case of large buildings, as in all developing nations, it is extremely difficult to achieve and to maintain architectural excellence in a furnished and used building because in most cases, even the users and the design objectives of the buildings change in time.

If this is to be regarded as axiomatic, then how are we going to achieve the longed for, high-quality physical environment I referred to at the beginning? The Awards, by making allocations of financial and technical resources, provide an invaluable opportunity in response to the problem, and represent a resource for architects and

AKAA, 1989, Institut du Monde Arabe

thinkers in the Muslim world. Their support would do much to further this important cause.

Doubtless, the arguments mentioned above express many legitimate concerns. It can be said that the criteria of the Award Program is always being further refined. Even though the awards presented in fields such as the restoration and improvement of conditions in squatter settlement areas are related to the built environment, the expansion of the Award to fields other than architects dilutes its influence. Perhaps, after the fifth cycle, the Program will seek to clarify some of these issues.

On the other hand, I believe that keeping in mind the primary objective of the Award, contrary to some people's expectations, such outcomes should not be the cause of disappointment. The intent and the perspective of the Award have found widespread support, and have led to significant benefits in many areas. Our attempts to interpret our culture, with its inherent sense of modesty, simplicity and maturity, need not fall prey to an unreasonable coveting of fashionable forms in large-scale industrialised settings that often represent obstacles to a creative built environment for the future.

Registan Square, Samarkand

JOURNEY TO SAMARKAND

Representing Islam through its Architecture

Don Mowatt

Within the Uzbek town of Bukhara, next to the minaret standing stout like an inverted punctuation mark, is the Kalyan Mosque built in 1514. Students from all over Central Asia are studying here and in the neighbouring Madrasah. As I wander through the gallery on one side of the mosque, I hear the voice of a teenage boy chanting verses from the Qu'ran. I turn on my tape recorder and go closer to the source. I can clearly hear the soulful chant as I stand beside a closed classroom door. After a moment, a small boy comes by and watches for a minute, then gestures for me to go inside, but I indicate my preference to be discrete and remain outside. He finds a chair for me and, after checking that my recorder is still turned on, signals to the older boy to resume his chant. It is a simple act of a small child done without thought for remuneration or reward, symbolising much in a culture where symbol and metaphor stand for a great deal. In a place where there had been much teaching, contemporary lessons are still possible.

Later that evening in a Samarkand hotel, Mohamed Arkoun, Professor of the History of Islamic Thought at the Sorbonne in Paris, explained his phrase 'A Space for Freedom'. He related the story of his own spiritual journey from his native Algeria to France as a student in the 1950s, struggling for political freedom, but finding it only much later in life. As we sat on a balcony overlooking the exquisite fifteenth-century turquoise dome of Cur-Emir, the resting place of Tamerlane and his grandson Ulug Beg, preparations were being made a few blocks away for the fifth cycle of the Aga Khan Architectural Awards.

This ancient city in a new republic was a particularly happy choice for an international architectural award ceremony. Bukhara is made up of four cities, all of which miraculously survive side by side from the Marakanda of Alexander the Great's time to the Samarkand of Genghis Khan in 1200, the medieval city of Tamerlane in 1400 when 2,300 resided here, to the contemporary 'Soviet' city. The buildings from each period stand tall and majestic, both aloof from, and also part of, the twentieth-century noise and bustle of a vital city. It was also a fitting location to talk about freedom as it is a capital that was the frequent home of conqueror and conquered.

Freedom, as Arkoun described it, involves the capacity to contend with all the contemporary problems in Muslim society without ever touching the ideological debates that have so divided Islam and alienated the West. This freedom for him had been attained through the totalising ability of architecture to address itself to issues of environment, urbanisation, cultural heritage and revitalisation. Architecture had become a metaphor for complete change through renewal.

My position as a radio documentarian was to follow this metaphor, and make sense of it for a radio audience in the West who could not see the buildings I would describe, nor be able to draw upon a common cultural heritage to assist them in visualising the unseen. Allegory and metaphor are common devices for expressing theological truths. However, what can be a clever turn of phrase in a philosophical discussion can be of painful annoyance to even a sympathetic radio audience unaccustomed to the cultural components revealed in the course of a series on Muslim architecture. Hence, it was of utmost importance that my own education in this unfamiliar field should be extensive, profound and immediate. It would obviously never be complete, nor I supposed, even adequate.

Bruno Freschi, the architect of the Ismaili Centre and Jamatkhana in Burnaby, near Vancouver, which was completed in 1985 as the first Ismaili Muslim building of its kind in Canada, offered his own paradoxical metaphor to the subject. 'In this building', he said, 'I want you to go into it in order that you might leave it – that is the nature of prayer after all'.

To me it became a driving metaphor for both my series and my understanding of the Islamic World. And the Burnaby Jamatkhana, less than a mile from the Danish Lutheran Church where I served as a deacon, became a kind of home base for my journey on the golden road to Samarkand through the world of Islamic architecture.

Once again, using both metaphor and paradox, we become aware of the significance of a contemporary building in the Far West, expressing to its users and neighbours alike the values of a religious and cultural tradition far removed in time and place, yet current and relevant. The Jamatkhana building itself is clad in Italian pietra etrusca dorata, a warm beige sandstone that reminds you of buildings and landscapes in the Middle East. The great portal entrance facing the Persian courtland announces its oneness with its traditions of domed

FROM ABOVE: Masjid-i Jami, Kalyan, Bukhara; Registan Square, Samarkand

mosques but also its individuality and thoroughly contemporary economy of form. In a neighbourhood of already-dated apartment and office buildings which were built after the Jamatkhana, it stands timeless and secure.

A recent series on American public television, 'The Power and the Glory', and a major series of articles in *The Vancouver Sun* both addressed the subject of Muslim fundamentalism. These were the focus of public perception of events in the Muslim world, a rising tide of protest, rejection and often violence, that evoked an enraged and unstable Muslim world. The fact, of course, is that this is a partial and often distorted representation of a very diverse and complex Muslim world, which is neither monolithic in its religious and cultural manifestations, nor susceptible to trite generalisations. Architecture would provide me with an alternative language to understand the heritage of Muslims and their contemporary concerns. It was visual, yet grounded in the intellectual and cultural concerns that had shaped Muslim spaces over the past one-and-a-half thousand years or so, and could once again be a vehicle for transforming society.

My first series of interviews was gathered in Boston at MIT, where John de Monchaux, an Australian architect who had moved to the United States, had assumed leadership of a faculty that had instituted a programme designed to train architects in the principles of Muslim architecture.

In the three decades following World War II, graduates of Western architectural schools who had come from the Middle East, returned with notions of modernism that had no felicitous application to their own cultures. So Islamic architecture around the world began to have a similarity to British, European and American architecture of the same period. The Aga Khan Program for Islamic Architecture at Harvard and MIT was designed in 1979 to counteract this trend. Specifically, the intentions were:

1 To maintain and improve at the two universities the teaching of the history of Islamic art and architecture and professional education in architecture and urban design for Islamic societies.

2 To promote thinking and research in all fields pertinent to a better understanding of Islamic architecture and urbanism, and to a creative and sensitive interpretation of this inheritance in contemporary environments.

3 To encourage Western and Islamic academic institutions and professionals to be aware of the achievements and the values of the Muslim past, and of the issues confronting Islamic societies today, and to develop means to strengthen that awareness.

Professor de Monchaux was an important first contact for me. His lucid, poetic descriptions of architectural principles as they applied to Muslim settings and traditions were not only fascinating but were expressed in a language that was particularly suited to radio. He too was heading for Samarkand for the first time – Samarkand, the unattainable as we had both grown up hearing it described. Again, as he said, an appropriate metaphor for architects who imagine something never yet seen.

Before going to Samarkand, I stopped in Paris and deliberately stayed in a hotel next to the Institute du Monde Arabe – a building recognised and awarded one of the Aga Khan Prizes in 1990. As it turned out, the hotel was also the one Swedish playwright August Strindberg lived in during his 'Inferno Crisis' at the end of the last century. This was very fortuitous as I was working on a radio series on the life and theatre of Strindberg at the same time as the Islamic series. Strindberg was involved in alchemy in the 1890s – a metaphysical pursuit as much devoted to transforming science into art as it was to turning base metal into gold. Another appropriate metaphor for my architectural project, I thought.

It was here I interviewed French architect Patrick Berger, one of the winners of the 1992 Samarkand Competition devised by local authorities, yet supported and administered by the Aga Khan Trust for Culture, to devise a new space in central Samarkand to incorporate the old monuments. I had known Berger since he and his wife were architectural assistants studying with Arthur Erickson in Vancouver in the early seventies. To Berger, it was essential to recognise that fashionable architecture would be as wrong in this setting as a nostalgic architecture. For him the connecting point between the two disparate worlds of medieval Samarkand and the city of the future was silence. Now this is radio language. Silence has become one of the rarest commodities in contemporary broadcasting, but a most valuable one. His vision of a modern city landscape was informed by images of Greece and Rome, where theatre and politics were conducted in public spaces surrounded by silence. The silence of the environment and the silence of time.

It was a point picked up by Mohamed Arkoun. After seeing the mausoleums, the madrasahs and the mosques in Samarkand, he was saddened and frustrated – not by the fact that they had not been well preserved or restored (some had been so very successfully) but by what he referred to as the emptiness and the lack of content. In Berger's reconstruction of Samarkand, the silence was to be a space around the ancient structures, allowing us to approach them with purpose and respect. For Arkoun, the quietness of the monuments today was a negative silence due to a loss of purpose and questionable respect; buildings had become remnants, not spaces of activity, scholarship and prayer that they were built for.

The passionate pleas for a rebirth of culture and context in the old sites perfectly complemented the awards made in Samarkand to projects that gave the poor in Muslim societies new dignity in spaces that they had begun to have a hand in shaping and rebuilding. Examples in Amman, Jordan, Yogyakarta and Indonesia were particularly striking in the way wretched living quarters had been turned by a government department in the first instance, and individual initiative in the second, into sound and imaginative housing complexes.

The individual in the case of the small urban project in Djakarta had been a Roman Catholic priest. In a country with a ninety per cent Muslim population, that seemed to me a very special lesson of cooperation, perfectly set in a space for freedom. It reminded me of the story told by the Indonesian Minister of Religious Affairs about the eastern region of his country: 'in the region of Maleku', he explained, 'the tolerance between the adherents of various faiths had reached such a level that if a Muslim section of the community is building a mosque, it is then exclusively the right of the Christian section to fix the roof of the mosque. On the other hand, if the Christian community is building a church, nobody can question the right of the Muslims to finish the floor of the church'.

I hope it will also be plausible within the concept of the totalising effect of architecture, that a deacon in the Danish Lutheran Church can tell the story on Canadian radio of this new space for Islam,[1] a space where reconstruction and redirection in the Muslim world can also benefit us in the non-Muslim world with its special gifts of creative silence and positive action.

NOTE

1 A three-hour programme entitled, *A New Space for Islam*, produced by Don Mowatt, was broadcast on CBS Radio in March 1993.

COURAGEOUS CRITERIA

Peter Davey

Within a world of architectural values which is becoming increasingly trivialised and marginalised, architectural criticism seems more and more preoccupied with external appearance and style. The profession itself is moving towards limitations dictated by external decoration around hulks of accommodation, the forms and spaces are determined by the development process and the building industry.

Architecture has a much nobler role. It is essentially a means of enhancing human life by the application of artistic imagination, rather than a method of simply heightening corporate profits and profile. This essence has never been forgotten by the Aga Khan Award. It is given triennially after careful investigation of buildings in use to discover how they work constructionally, socially and economically. With few exceptions, it has never been given to buildings just because they are fashionable or held in high esteem by the critical community.

They are the only awards that are given over such a wide geographical and social spectrum. They range in scope from improvements worked on some of the worst slums in the world to expensive tourist developments. Geographically, they span the huge Muslim world which stretches from Morocco to the Moluccas, and Samarkand to Sumatra. In the temporal dimension, they cover restoration work on some of the best loved ancient monuments like the al-Aqsa Mosque to modern office blocks.

The main problem that the awards have confronted is the difficulty of finding a set of criteria that can comprehend such diversity. At one time, this seemed to be impossible. We argued that the awards should be divided into distinct divisions: for instance, slum improvements and the restoration of old work and contemporary commercial buildings. This plan was followed in some cases, and up to a point it served well by highlighting the many dimensions covered by the scheme.

This year's awards have thrown out such categorisations. The jury members have bravely decided to try to set a criterion whereby all the work reviewed, wherever it may be from, and whoever it may be for, can be looked at simultaneously. In doing so, they have challenged us all to reconsider the nature of architectural judgement.

After a couple of decades of style worship, such a criterion is difficult to articulate but is best summed up by the end of the preamble to the jury's report (Selma al-Radi and Charles Moore) which says that it sought 'economically sustainable, humanistic solutions . . . relevant for the developed countries as well as the developing world'.

In detailed judgements, much stress is laid on ecological appropriateness. All the designs recognised by the Award have used local materials in economical but imaginative ways; all have been aware of the need to conserve energy and reduce pollution in an increasingly despoiled planet.

All the prize-winning buildings have been chosen as being easy to replicate, not as exact forms, but as models of how good building can be created within particular societies. And they set examples of how traditional craftsmanship can be adapted and made relevant to contemporary technology and ways of life. From the team of masons and scholars who are reopening the palaces of Istanbul to the earth builders of Burkina Faso, disciplines are being set up that can be used on future work.

The vast variety of the Islamic world is reflected in the way in which the prize-winning work makes very different particular places appropriate to local cultures. This time, there are no pastiche attempts to capture the past (as there were when Robert Venturi was a juror in 1986). Instead, the chosen buildings draw on custom, craft and climate to make places that resonate, rather than reflect, the past.

The jury's concern to find building of 'directness and modesty' which 'have lessons for the world at large' has possibly precluded the inclusion of large commercial and bureaucratic buildings that enhance ordinary life. Perhaps they do not exist in the Islamic world; perhaps they are only made in the West by exceptional clients and architects. The criteria used by this jury should enable the next one to search for such work. If it can be found, the debate generated by the Aga's awards will affect our lives in every dimension.

Courtesy of the author and Architectural Review, *No 50.*

OPPOSITE: Panafrican Institute for Development, Ouagadougou, Burkina Faso

1992 Award Master Jury. Bottom row, left to right: S Zulficar, BV Doshi, A Shuaibi, F Maki, F Gehry; Middle row, L to R: R Holod, D Tekeli, A Nanji; Top row, L to R: A Moersid, S Özkan

TALK BY HIS HIGHNESS THE AGA KHAN AT THE UIA/AIA CONGRESS OF ARCHITECTS

18TH JUNE 1993

Distinguished guests, Ladies and Gentlemen, to speak to the World Congress of Architects is a special privilege. I am honoured to be with you today, especially as this meeting is one of the most important gatherings of architects the world has ever seen. I am daunted by the task of talking to such a distinguished and unprecedented audience.

Let me say how deeply I share the conviction of the organisers of this Congress that architects have a critical and subtle role to play in moving the world towards a sustainable society. Indeed it is my very faith – Islam – which articulates that concept. God has entrusted his world to the living, in order that we may improve it from one generation to the next. This is the ethic which must govern our actions in relation to the physical world around us. Thus, our spiritual, cultural and institutional capacity, as well as the earth's physical and natural resources become our legacy, a legacy which we must pass on to future generations.

For these, but also for other reasons – at least three – I have an abiding interest in architecture. Firstly, issues of development are central to my concerns and responsibilities. The institutions with which I am involved seek to light the flame of human opportunity in the poorest areas of Asia and Africa. These parts of our world face extraordinary pressures of constraint. The issues are truly humbling. Buildings, spaces, settlements and cities are forceful factors in the development process. The qualities they have – or can be given – enable or confine opportunity. Buildings lead or mislead by their example. The qualities we give them are therefore an essential link in the chain that leads to expanded human opportunity.

Secondly, the development of sustainable environments draws not only on the physical resources of a society but also upon the cultural and artistic resources that shape the values of that society. Buildings, spaces, settlements and cities are the embodiment and bearer of those values. In 1986 the masterful rehabilitation of the old town of Mostar was recognised by the Aga Khan Award for Architecture. From a lifeless relic of an historic past, the city thrived culturally and exploded in economic opportunity. The rebuilding of Mostar illustrated how powerfully cultural continuity contributes to human well-being. In today's tragic Yugoslavia, death has returned to Mostar.

Undoubtedly, architecture will carry cultural values from one generation to the next. I must therefore seek to understand architecture if I am to address the processes of change, orderly or disorderly, in contemporary society – and especially so in the dynamic and diverse settings of the Muslim world.

Thirdly, I have been involved, since the death of my grandfather in 1957, extensively, and in person, in the building process. It was then that I began to observe, in depth, what was being built in the developing world. Hospitals, schools, housing and commercial buildings were – and unfortunately still are – being built with an unthinking allegiance to what I might call the 'Footsteps' credo. This credo implied that there was a single path to be taken in social *and* architectural development, a path already trodden in the First World. I came to believe that this path deserved to be questioned on many grounds: cultural, social, economic and aesthetic. It was also dubious whether this path would lead to the goal of sustainability.

The questions were clear and precise, but the answers had to be sought from a series of ventures into the unknown. The Aga Khan Award for Architecture, the Program for Islamic Architecture at Harvard and MIT, and the Historic Cities Support Program of Trust for Culture were created to analyse the issues and search for answers. Their goal is – simply – to have a positive impact on the quality of buildings, spaces, settlements and cities throughout the world, but particularly in the Muslim World.

What have we learnt so far? Certainly, the first important lesson is that efforts to create a humane, sustainable environment must focus more urgently and positively on rural areas in the developing world. Throughout Asia and Africa the overwhelming bulk of the population live and build in rural areas. In a changing world, the choices these people are going to be able to make will have a profound impact on the ecology of the planet. It is *others* who are making choices today, and the impact of those choices is devastating. It is urgent and essential that these choices should be made in a way which respect a people's legitimate claim to a better life, whilst remaining sensitive to the ecology of their setting. I truly believe that these two sets of demands can be reconciled in harmony.

We have ample evidence in our work in rural areas in

FROM ABOVE: 1980 Aga Khan Award ceremony venue, Shalimar Garden, Lahore, Pakistan; 1986 Aga Khan Award ceremony venue, Badi Palace, Marrakesh, Morocco; 1989 Aga Khan Award ceremony venue, The Citadel, Cairo, Egypt

India and Pakistan that this can be done. For the sustainable development of a rural economy and its environment, access to education and professional expertise *and* the energy and motivation of the people involved, are required. Sustainable development in the Third World requires an accessible understanding of a process of change that is without precedent in the experience of its people. There is a clear need that the choice of local people be informed and not compelled.

For such a process to be sustained, those taking part must view it as a priority in their lives. They must be able to see identifiable benefits as a result of their participation. And they must be able to take part in the process at a cost they can afford.

Architects, planners, economists and experts in agriculture, hydrology, geology, forestry and other fields must find ways to work together with – and on behalf of – the people of rural areas, to develop an anticipatory process for the development of the physical environment. By such a process I mean one in which a rigorous exchange leads to practical solutions that reconcile ecological, economic, social and cultural demands.

Too often the physical problems associated with the development have been thought to be relatively simple, and not deserving of the same level of attention given, deservedly, to issues of health, literacy or economic development. We must not displace the attention given to these issues. Rather we should recognise that physical development problems are complex, pervasive and insidious in their impact. As such they deserve a clear place in development priorities, policies and higher education. They also deserve far greater attention in the primary and secondary curricula.

In our work we have learned that the quality of a built environment will almost always be a reflection of the respect and stewardship given to material resources. Quality can also be found in the elegance and fit of the trade-offs made when conflicting demands arise between one realm of resource and another. Those who build and those who advise them in that task will make these choices and trade-offs on the basis of the ethnic and social values they hold. We have learned that there are sometimes deep and significant differences in their values. These differences need to be open to debate. Debate and enquiry in architects enlarge their share of responsibility for the quality of the built environment. Enquiry must reach across all dimensions of architecture. The economic, technical, cultural and aesthetic dimensions of buildings all demand our attention and deep understanding.

What else are we learning? For the first time, from the Award for Architecture, we are beginning to see that buildings and places can be created in ways that reconcile – with elegance – the different demands of sustainability. Never before have we seen so many new buildings of social purpose, small schools and medical centres of real quality, in rural villages that set such a remarkable standard. The judgements of the 1992 Award Jury, for example, hold some crucial lessons for an architecture that will support a sustainable world. The evident combination of dignity, aptness and modesty that is found in each of the winning projects points to an architecture that is competent, caring and subtle in its call upon resources.

However, we have learned that it is impractical, even misleading, to imagine that an architect's services will be employed to guide more than the smallest fraction of the additions made every year to the world's stock buildings.

There are those who would say that the profession is irrelevant to the mass of building taking place in the world. I firmly believe otherwise. I urge you to take up the deliberate responsibility to guide by example and by precept. Your few works must give examples to the millions who build without architects every year. You must show, by example, how self-built rural housing in Central Asia can be built to withstand the devastation of earthquakes; how a backstreet factory in Senegal can meet acceptable environmental standards for those who work there; or how the design of a community's school in Java can enhance and dignify the learning experience.

Do not only set the example, share it in a generous and deliberate way, so that it reaches all those who build in every part of the world. Your skills have a meaning and an impact which can become vital. The results of your efforts – for good and ill – are felt far beyond the responses of your clients or your peers. This impact is a challenge without precedent or parallel, to your profession and to its schools. The challenge is for all to raise, through the thoughtful practice of your profession, the well-being of the planet and its people of today and tomorrow. There are a series of specific questions I urge you to take up to meet this challenge:

– Because there is nothing so powerful as tested knowledge and judgement, I urge you to ask *how you can better learn from each other* in debate and constructive criticism.

– Because you are privileged with this knowledge, I urge you to ask *how you can share what you learn*, by deliberate efforts, *with the many millions who will build without the benefit of an architect's advice.*

– Because your actions will set standards and expectations, I urge you to imagine that your example will be followed by millions of others who build in this world –

and therefore to ask *how you can exercise greater care in setting that example.*

– Because we share the burden of stewardship of the earth, please ask *how the design and technology of buildings can minimise the call on non-renewable resources.*

– Because the resources we pass on to future generations are cultural as well as material, I urge you to ask *how better to recognise and honour the requirement that both be enriched,* and finally,

– Because the most pressing environmental and human risks are to be found in the developing world, *I urge you to turn a serious part of your attention to questions confronting the creation of the built environment in that world*: to rural areas where the greatest risks to the world's ecology and human opportunity reside; and to the great and small cities that will emerge in the twenty-first century, where enterprises must be guided with far greater respect to physical and cultural resources than this century has shown.

For my own part I am committed to the same challenge and to address the same questions which I urge upon you. I shall continue to work with architects and the communities and clients they serve throughout the world (especially in the Muslim world). And I shall seek to develop new understandings and interventions that might enable the people in rural and urban areas in Asia and Africa to take a more informed and sensitive command of their environment and social development. In all of these activities I will seek your ideas, your support and your critical participation.

In these endeavours we must together seek to strengthen and enrich the dialogue in which we account for the consequences of our actions as makers of buildings, spaces, settlements and cities. And we must together enlarge the freedom that will enable that dialogue to take place. Architecture and its concerns need to become a staple topic in the lives of millions more people in the world today. Such attention will be earned by your actions and your advocacy. It will stem from the evidence that your buildings and your teaching lead to the conservation and revitalisation of the earth's resources. If you ensure that your work sustains these resources, your standards will become an imperative that the world will not ignore.

Thank you for the opportunity to raise these questions.

ANOTHER MOORE

Hasan-Uddin Khan

Charles Moore was an enigmatic figure of contemporary architecture. I can think of very few architects who were as busy as he was over the past decade – 'stretched to the limit' is a phrase that comes to mind. His long and important involvement with architecture and teaching is well known but what is not was his interest and contribution to the architecture of Islamic and developing countries, mainly through the Aga Khan Award for Architecture, a relationship that began in the early 1980s. A scholarly and more exhaustive article should be written abut this, but at this moment of remembering Charles and his work, perhaps a few anecdotes are the best way in which to record it, and the sense of humour that was his hallmark.

If I remember correctly, it was Mildred Schmertz, then with *Architectural Record*, who suggested that the Award contact Charles Moore. She suggested that as Charles was always travelling, the best opportunity to make his acquaintance would be on a trip with him: which is how she herself began to know him. Like most people, she enjoyed his wit and sense of the absurd, and recounts how, when on a bus together in Yemen on the way to visit a town called Hadja, a fellow passenger asked, 'Where is Hadja?' Moore promptly answered, 'Five minutes from Gotcha!'

Moore's real interest in the architecture of non-Western cultures had been a long-standing one from an academic and touristic viewpoint – South-East Asia being one of his favourite regions – but a more systematic involvement came with the invitation from the Aga Khan Award to become a member of its Master Jury in 1981. (The Award, one recalls, is the triennial prize of $500,000, selected by an independent master jury, and is given to winning works that make a contribution to the contemporary architecture of the Muslim world.) Moore, with his usual enthusiasm, accepted and immersed himself in the task of looking at the architectural production of a set of buildings which he tried to understand as an outsider. This indeed became his strength and contribution: to examine architecture of another culture, to not only judge 'good design', for which he had strong views, but also to understand the cultural contexts and means of production, be it from the craft tradition or that of modern technology. His willingness to understand different design approaches, and his personal standing as an architect, brought to the decisions of that 1983 set of Awards a sympathetic evaluation of smaller projects based on indigenous models that might well have been overlooked otherwise. One such project was the Cakirhan holiday house in the Akyaka area of Turkey, designed using the vernacular, not by an architect but by a poet. The Secretary-General of the Award, Suha Özkan, told Charles that this decision would be most controversial in

Turkey because it was not in the modern image and that it had been designed by a non-architect in a folklore manner. Charles commented that this then would be even more important as a lesson because it would signal that local values and traditions could produce elegant buildings which related to their contexts and lifestyles better than those seen as 'high design'. Charles understood, perhaps intuitively, that good architecture and its reflections of culture were important and not necessarily the result of professional interventions. How this is reflected in his own architecture is another story.

Moore was also fascinated by, and admired His Highness the Aga Khan's vision and efforts to improve the quality of life for Muslims throughout the world and to express new, appropriate and contemporary architecture. From 1987 to 1992, Charles served as a member of the Award's Steering Committee – the body that oversees the Award's policy and concerns. Diligently he attended all the meetings in Geneva and several of its international seminars. On one occasion, after a long day of meetings he was having dinner at the exclusive Hotel Richmond's dining room with Muhammad Yunus, the Chairman of the Bangladeshi Grameen Bank and a fellow Steering Committee member. (The Grameen Bank is an extraordinary institution which provides loans to the poorest sectors of the Bangladeshi population, and mainly to women, to help improve their living conditions through the development of a simple kit of parts to build stable homes.) Yunus, whose concerns were with people and building at a very basic level, could not help remarking that the dinner they were having could probably house two families in Bangladesh using the kit that they had developed. Charles, who was interested in housing and housing standards and costs, expressed his concern and began to reconsider some of his own perspectives on the subject – as did Yunus.

For a seminar to be held on housing in Zanzibar in the autumn of 1988, Charles and I were to make a presentation on the importance of the individual house to the architecture of the Third World, where informal sector and mass housing and planning were considered the major issues. It was unfortunately the time when he had just a heart operation and we had to develop the theme of the presentation over the phone. He made just three points which I incorporated into the presentation. He observed that single family houses in the late twentieth century seem possible only for the very rich and the poor – everyone else is expected to fit into anonymous slab blocks. He stressed the importance of the indigenous house as being one that is 'an extension of the human body, an outer layer of clothing, not altogether like other people' but capable of accommodating self-expression and lets its occupants inhabit it'. He also recounted how some seventeen years earlier he had taken a class of architecture students to Istanbul to look at dwellings made by people who could have exactly what they wanted. He asked his students to return to the USA to rewrite the minimum property standards of the American Federal Housing Authority, but the experiment did not work – most of the students never did see the connection and he decided not to push this analogy further. In conclusion he called for a reappraisal of housing when he said, 'sixty years ago cities seemed airless and Le Corbusier dreamed of skyscrapers in the parks. We have learned to do the skyscrapers but the parks have eluded us . . . we can dig into traditional memory to try and find in our new programmes the intimate scale, the variety and the complexity, the qualities of the single family house that will give a chance for the inhabitants of mass housing truly to inhabit their dwellings'.

Charles always had time for students and young architects and on several occasions he talked about his work to the young in the Third World. Not much of a public speaker, he would pepper his presentations with images which made interesting and thoughtful connections with history and other works, giving everyone food for thought.

I remember the time he gave to the architectural journal *Mimar: Architecture in Development*, which I edited. He first contributed to it in 1983 – without being paid anything because he believed in what we were trying to do. Years later he hosted a few of us in his house at Sea Ranch on the Californian coastline where we were judging a student competition for the publication. 'It never ceases to amaze me', he said, 'just how strange and impractical each generation of student work can be'. Then he chuckled, 'but I guess that many people think that of my work today!' Those few days and later occasions spent with him in Austin and elsewhere were always good fun and memorable.

The last time he came to Geneva he spent a couple of weeks at the Trust's offices writing up, with his colleague Selma Al-Radi, project descriptions for the 1992 Award book, published by Academy Group, entitled, *Architecture for a Changing World*, bringing to bear his wise observations and extracting the elements of projects he felt important to stress in communicating Award winners to a general and wide public. He remained generous with his time to the concerns of Islamic architecture (which seemed to find some resonance with his own sense of the varied use of materials and colours) even though he had – and expected – no commissions in these regions. He always said that the Award gave him a rich set of unusual experiences, the last of which was his visit to the venue of the Award ceremony in Samarkand in September

1992. By then he moved slowly and with difficulty, but he gamely visited the sites with other participants, took delight in seeing new things and people and kept up his good-humoured banter even when he was so unwell.

When Charles passed away last December, those in the Islamic world who had been touched by his presence felt his loss; others simply knew him as one of the major twentieth-century architectural figures. And in the West, where his work is located and best known, little do people realise the warmth and affection with which he was held in cultures remote from his own and the contributions made by his open-minded view of different architectures. He was an architect regarded with much fondness by those who knew him, and to paraphrase a eulogy of many years ago, 'May God keep him and enjoy him as much as we did'.

CONTRIBUTORS

Professor Azim Nanji was born in Nairobi, Kenya and educated in Kenya, Tanzania, Makerere University in Uganda, receiving his MA and PhD from McGill Univeristy. He taught at both Canadian and American univerisities and was the Margaret Gest Professor for the Cross-Cultural Study of Religion at Haverford College, Pennsylvania. He is currently Professor and Chair of the Department of Religion at the University of Florida. He has travelled widely in Africa, Asia, Australia, Europe and North America. Dr Nanji is Co-Chair of the Islam Section at the American Academy of Religion and a member of the Council on Foundations Committee on Religions and Philanthropy. He served as a member of the Master Jury for the Aga Khan Award in 1992. He is author, editor and contributor to various works on religion, Islam and Ismailism.

Dr Jamel Akbar is an architect and urban designer and was born in Taif, Saudi Arabia. He received his BA from King Saud University, Riyadh, and his M Arch, AS and PhD from MIT. He is the author of *Crisis in the Built Environment: The Case of the Muslim City*, and an Arabic book entitled *Imarat al-Ard fi al-Islam*, as well as many articles. He is currently an Associate Professor at King Faisal University, Damman, Saudi Arabia and the Chairman of the Board of 'al-Umran Association', an association for designers and environmentalists.

Dr Mohammed Al-Asad received his PhD in Islamic Architecture from Harvard in 1990. He has taught and held post-doctoral posts at the Institute for Advanced Studies, the School of Historical Studies, Princeton University, Harvard University and MIT, and is currently supervising the establishment of a Graduate Institute for the Study of Art and Architecture of the Islamic World at Al-al Bayt University in Jordan.

Nader Ardalan is Principal, Senior Vice President and Director of Design, Interiors and New York Projects at Jung/Brannen Associates Inc, as well as President of Nader Ardalan and Associates in Boston. He had been Visiting Professor at Harvard, Yale and MIT. His projects are as diverse as the places in which they are located: California and Rhode Island, Iran Kuwait, Saudi Arabia and Turkey to name a few. Ardalan was founding member of the Aga Khan Award for Architecture Steering Committee and has received numerous honours and awards.

Professor Mohammed Arkoun, an academician of Algerian origin is Professor Emeritus of History of Islamic Thought at the Sorbonne. He has been a Visiting Professor at several universities in the United States, Europe and the Muslim world. Professor Arkoun concentrates on classical Islam and contemporary issues of Islam facing modernity, and has published extensively in several languages. He is associated with several European initiatives to re-think and re-shape the relationship between Europe, Islam and the Mediterranean

World. Based in Paris and Amsterdam, he also serves as Senior Research Fellow at the Institute of Ismaili Studies in London. He has been associated with the Award from its founding and served on the Steering Committee until 1992.

Wayne Attoe is the author of six books on architecture and urban design. He taught at Louisiana State University, the University of Texas at Austin, the University of Wisconsin-Milwaukee, and has been a Visiting Professor at Oxford Polytechnic, England and the University of California, Berkeley. He lives in California.

Omar Bwana is Deputy Director of the National Museums of Kenya in Nairobia. He has represented Kenya in many international conferences and is the recipient of the German Order of Merit for his contribution to strengthening cultural relations. He has been active in preservation projects in Lamu and Mombasa, served as a Member of Parliament in the Kenya National Assembly from 1979-83, and serves on the Board of the Aga Khan Education Services in Kenya.

Dr Turgut Cansever is a Turkish architect, planner and art historian. In addition to university appointments in Turkey, he has extensive experience in directing, managing and advising local and state government institutions on urban development, housing, cultural and conservation projects. The recipient of three Aga Khan Awards for Architecture, he has received numerous other awards in his career and has been published extensively.

Peter Davey was born in England and is Editor of *Architectural Review*. He has taught and lectured on design at many British architectural schools in Paris, MIT and in Europe and Australia.

Professor Gulzar Haider, born in Lahore, Pakistan is an architect and Professor of Architecture at Carlton University in Ottawa, Canada. He is a member of the International Commission for the Preservation of Islamic Cultural Heritage (IRCICA) in Istanbul and served as a Member of the Organising Committe of the King Fahd Award for Design and Research in Islamic Architecture.

Dr Rafique Keshavjee, born in South Africa, obtained a PhD in Anthropology and Middle Eastern Studies at Harvard University. A Post-Doctoral Fellow at the Aga Khan Program for Islamic Architecture at MIT for three years, he then became Research Associate in the Graduate School of Design at Harvard. He examined and documented innovations in low-income housing in Asia and Africa and during much of this time was Vice Chairman of the Aga Khan Foundation, USA. He is currently an Associate Dean at the Institute of Ismaili Studies, London.

Hassan-Uddin Khan, born in Hyderabad, India is an architect. Besides serving as one of the initial Convenors of the Aga Khan Award for Architecture and a member of the Steering Committe (1981-89), he has been Director of Special Profects and Outreach for the the Aga Khan Trust for Culture and Editor-in-Chief of *Minar*. He is currently affiliated with the Harvard/MIT Aga Khan Program in Architecture, and serves on the Advisory Committe of the Getty Architectural Grant Program.

Professor Ronald Lewcock is an Australian architect, educator and former Aga Khan Professor of Architecture and Design in Islamic Studies at MIT, where he remains a visiting professor and Professor of Architecture at the Georgia Institute of Technology, USA. Professor Lewcock was a member of the Master Jury in 1986, and has written extensively on Islamic architecture, the conservation of buildings and urban rehabilitation.

Dr Don Mowatt is a Producer at the Canadian Broadcasting Corporation (CBC) in Vancouver, Canada. He has represented Canada at several major international conferences on the arts and has won numerous Canadian and American Awards. In 1990 he received the Lifetime Achievement Award from the Association for the Study of Canadian Radio and Television and in 1993 produced 'A New Space of Islam' for CBC radio.

Dr Suha Özkan was born in Ankara, Turkey, in 1945. He studied architecture at the Middle East Technical University (METU) in Ankara, and theory of design at the Architectural Association in London. Dr Özkan has undertaken extensive research on the theory and history of architecture, design, vernacular form and emergency housing, and has published numerous articles and monographs. At METU, he taught architectural design and design theory for fifteen years, and became associate dean of the faculty of architecture in 1978. In 1979, he was appointed vice president of the university. With the Aga Khan Award for Architecture in Geneva, Dr Özkan served as the deputy secretary-general from 1983 to 1990, and has been the secretary general since 1991.

Dr Ismail Serageldin, born in Egypt, is Vice President for Environmentally Sustainable Development at the World Bank. He has worked extensively in Sub-Saharan Africa, North Africa, Europe and the Middle East. Within the bank he has specialised in designing and managing poverty-focused projects in the developing countries. He is a widely published author on economic development and human resource issues with the Arab world, Islam, culture, architecture and urbanism. He was a member of the Steering Committe of the Awards (1986-92) and a member of the Master Jury in 1983.

His excellency, the late **Dr Soedjatmoko**, an historian and sociologist served Indonesia in many capacities, including acting as the Ambassador to the United States. He was also Rector of the United Nations University in Tokyo and a member of the Award Master Jury in 1980.

Dr Dogan Tekeli, a Turkish architect, has lectured architectural design at the Macka School of Architecture, and engineering at the Istanbul Technical University. He was President of the Chamber of Turkish Architects for one term in 1957. Tekeli and his partner have won more than twenty design competitions in Turkey. He was consultant to the Municipiality of Istanbul (1985-88), is a member of the board of the Turkish Association of Consulting Engineers and Architects and has served on the Award Steering Committee.

MEMBERS OF THE MASTER JURIES 1980-92

Esin Atil, Rasem Badran, Geoffrey Bawa, Titus Burckhardt, Turgut Cansever, Sherban Cantacuzino, Rifat Chadirji, Charles Correa, Giancarlo de Carlo, Kamran Diba, Balkrishna Doshi, Abdel Wahed el-Wakil, Mahdi Elmandjra, Habib Fida-Ali, Frank Gehry, Oleg Grabar, Mahbub ul-Haq, Hans Hollein, Renata Holod, Saad Eddin Ibrahim, Muzharul Islam, Zahir Ud-deen Khwaja, Mübeccel Kiray, Aptullah Kuran, Ronald Lewcock, Fumihiko Maki, Adhi Moersid, Charles Moore, Azim Nanji, Mehmet Doruk Pamir, Hasan Poerbo, William Porter, Ismail Serageldin, Mona Serageldin, Ali Shuaibi, Roland Simounet, Soedjatmoko, James Stirling, Kenzo Tange, Dogan Tekeli, Robert Venturi, Parid Wardi bin Sudin, Saïd Zulficar.

MEMBERS OF THE STEERING COMMITTEES 1980-95

Selma al-Radi, Nader Ardalan, Mohammed Arkoun, Garr Campbell, Sherban Cantacuzino, Sir Hugh Casson, Charles Correa, John de Monchaux, Hassan Fathy, Sir Bernard Feilden, Frank Gehry, Oleg Grabar, Arif Hasan, Renata Holod, Hasan-Uddin Khan, Dogan Kuban, Ronald Lewcock, Nurcholish Madjid, Mohamed Makiya, Charles Moore, Kamil Khan Mumtaz, William Porter, Ismail Serageldin, Ali Shuaibi, Dogan Tekeli, Muhammad Yunus.

AWARDS LIST

1980

Kampung Improvement Programme, Jakarta, Indonesia
Pondok Pesantren Pabelan, Central Java, Indonesia
Ertegün House, Bodrum, Turkey
Turkish Historical Society, Ankara, Turkey
Mughal Sheraton Hotel, Agra, India
Sidi Bou Saïd, Tunis, Tunisia
Rustëm Pasa Caravanserai, Erdine, Turkey
National Museum, Doha, Qatar
Ali Qapu, Chehel Sutun and Hasht Behesht, Isfahan, Iran
Halawa House, Agamy, Egypt
Medical Centre, Mopti, Mali
Courtyard Houses, Agadir, Morocco
Inter-Continental Hotel and Conference Centre, Mecca, Saudi Arabia
Water Towers, Kuwait City, Kuwait
Agricultural Training Centre, Nianing, Senegal
Chairman's Award: Hassan Fathy

1983

The Great Mosque of Niono, Niono, Mali
Sherefudin's White Mosque, Visoko, Yugoslavia
Ramses Wissa Wassef Arts Centre, Giza, Egypt
Nail Cakirhan Residence, Akyaka Village, Turkey
Hafsia Quarter, Tunis, Tunisia
Tanjong Jara Beach Hotel and Rantau Abang Visitor's Centre, Kuala Trengganu, Malaysia
Residence Andalous, Sousse, Tunisia
The Hajj Terminal, Jeddah, Saudi Arabia
Tomb of Shah Rukh-i-'Alam, Multan, Pakistan
Darb Qirmiz, Cairo, Egypt
The Azem Palace, Damascus, Syria

1986

The Social Security Complex, Istanbul, Turkey
Dar Lamane Housing Community, Casablanca, Morocco
The Conservation of Mostar Old Town, Mostar, Yugoslavia
The Restoration of al-Aqsa Mosque, al-Haram al-Sharif, Jerusalem
Yaama Mosque, Yaama, Tahoua, Niger
Bhong Mosque, Bhong Rahim Yar Khan, Pakistan

Honourable Mentions
Shushtar New Town, Shushtar, Iran
Improvement of Kampung Kebalen, Surabaya, Indonesia
Ismaïliyya Development Project, Ismailiyya, Egypt
Saïd Naum Mosque, Jakarta, Indonesia
Historic Sites Development, Istanbul, Turkey
Chairman's Award: Rifat Chadirji

1989

Restoration of the Great Omari Mosque, Sidon, Lebanon
Rehabilitation of Asilah, Asilah, Morocco
Grameen Bank Housing Programme, various locations in Bangladesh
Citra Niaga Urban Development, Samarinda, East Kalimantan, Indonesia
Gürel Family Summer Residence, Canakkale, Turkey
Hayy Assafarat Landscaping and Al Kindi Plaza, Riyadh, Saudi Arabia
Sidi el-Aloui Primary School, Tunis, Tunisia
Corniche Mosque, Jeddah, Saudi Arabia
Ministry of Foreign Affairs, Riyadh, Saudi Arabia
National Assembly Building, Sher-e-Bangla Nagar, Dhaka, Bangladesh
Institut du Monde Arabe, Paris, France

1992

Kairouan Conservation Programme, Kairouan, Tunisia
Palace Parks Programme, Istanbul, Turkey
Cultural Park for Children, Cairo, Egypt
East Wahdat Upgrading Programme, Amman, Jordan
Kampung Kali Cho-de, Yogyakarta, Indonesia
Stone Building System, Dar'a Province, Syria
Demir Holiday Village, Bodrum, Turkey
Panafrican Institute for Development, Ouagadougou, Barkina Faso
Entrepreneurship Development Institute of India, Ahmedabad, India